KUNDALINI–

PSYCHOSIS OR TRANSCENDENCE?

Thesis   15, 30, 42, 97

KUNDALINI—

PSYCHOSIS OR TRANSCENDENCE?

Lee Sannella, M. D.

H. S. DAKIN COMPANY
3101 WASHINGTON STREET
SAN FRANCISCO, CA 94115

MEMBER
COSMEP
COMMITTEE OF SMALL MAGAZINE
EDITORS AND PUBLISHERS

ACKNOWLEDGEMENTS

This book is, to a large extent, the product of a group effort. In particular, the author and the publisher wish to thank Keith Borden, Freda Morris, Gabriel Cousens, Danniel Kientz, Jean Millay, Richard Lowenberg, Elaine Chernoff, Beverly Johnson, George Meek, James Fadiman, and Itzhak Bentov for their advice and assistance in preparing, editing, and reviewing the manuscript and artwork.

The participation of many other individuals in the research described here is gratefully acknowledged, although, for medical reasons, their names are not given.

CONTENTS

INTRODUCTION

Tissues are torn, blood vessels severed, blood spilled, much fluid is lost; the heart races and the blood pressure soars. There is moaning, crying, and screaming. A severe injury? No, only a relatively normal human birth. The description sounds pathological because the symptoms were not understood in relation to the outcome: a new human being.

In a darkened room a man sits alone. His body is swept by muscular spasms. Indescribable sensations and sharp pains run from his feet up his legs and over his back and neck. His skull feels as if it will burst. Inside his head he hears roaring sounds and high-pitched whistling. Then suddenly a sunburst floods his inner being. His hands burn. He feels his body tearing within. Then he laughs and is overcome with bliss.

A psychotic episode? No, this is a psycho-physiological transformation, a rebirth process as natural as physical birth. It seems pathological only because the symptoms are not understood in relation to the outcome: an enlightened human being.

When allowed to progress to completion this process culminates in deep psychological balance, strength, and maturity. Its initial stages, however, often share the violence, helplessness, and imbalance that attend the start of human infancy.

For thousands of years, from the ancient Vedas onward, this process has been described. Until recently, it was confined to distant cultures, esoteric traditions, and a few isolated individuals. Accounts of it have usually been highly personal and often permeated with vague mysticism and strange mythology. As a result, the accounts were not taken seriously and no systematic comparison of the reports from different traditions was possible. Also, many of these traditions claimed divine revelation and absolute truth. Consequently professionals have remained confused, skeptical and suspicious.

Lately, two factors have changed this situation radically. First, there has been a marked increase in the number of people undergoing intense spiritual experiences within our own culture (Greeley and McCready, 1975). Second, the influence of Western science has resulted in a new emphasis on describing the *objective* aspects of this process in other societies as well as our own. Consequently, it is now possible to compare the experiences of different traditions by a uniform set of standards and to apply those same standards in making first-hand clinical observations.

We find a marked uniformity in the descriptions of this process from widely disparate traditions. Gopi Krishna (1973), a Yogi writer, says that from the recorded experiences of Christian mystics, Sufi Masters, and yoga adepts, it is obvious that the basic essentials of the experience are the same. A study of these accounts, when enough detail is recorded, reveals symptom patterns and types of sensations that are similar to those found in our cases.

We believe that these common aspects have physiological components, and that activation of a single physiological mechanism is at the root of the wide diversity of phenomena we see. If these assumptions are correct, the idea of spiritual rebirth or enlightenment can no longer be considered a confusing jumble of superstitions, religious dogmas, and wild rumors. Spiritual rebirth has become, instead, a well-defined entity. We may now ask, what is this process? To what state does it lead? Do these people really develop psychic powers? How does it differ from normality, on the one hand, and from psychosis on the other? Is it merely another one of the altered states of consciousness that many researchers are now exploring, or is it something more?

It is not simply an altered state of consciousness, but an ongoing process, lasting from several months to many years, during which the person passes in and out of different states of consciousness. The process falls outside the categories of both normal and psychotic, because a person undergoing the transformation has

2

experiences far removed from normal, usually without becoming so disorganized as to be considered psychotic. Nor is the process simply one of becoming psychic, because persons who have not undergone the transformation may be psychic, while others who have completed it may not be. The transformation may lead to many special abilities, but it is not intrinsically tied to them. Tirtha (1962) points out that a great Yogi who has control over his heart action may not have his kundalini active, while one with an active kundalini may have no such abilities.

For the person undergoing the transformation, the significance of the enlightened state may be highly personal and subjective. Our aim, however, is to describe the process itself in terms of what can be observed.

In this book we present many cases, some from a survey of diverse cultures and spiritual traditions, and others from our own clinical experience. These give us ample data for composing a portrait of the process.

Ordinarily a clinician may present his or her cases with the expectation that they will be accepted at face value, although the conclusions may be questioned. But in this area we are forced to hesitate. Should we present data that appear impossible in the current models of Western science? Or should we refrain from publishing observations we believe to be accurate, in order not to jeopardize acceptance of more vital issues? We feel that holding back data is evasive and, in the long run, destructive to the spirit of science. If today's models prove inadequate, it is because tomorrow's will be better. Not only the researcher and the writer, but also the reader must here make a special effort to be objective.

We believe that the writers cited are reliable. Our own cases are all living, and, except for one, are currently in touch with the author. With a few exceptions, they are willing to be interviewed by any serious investigator. Researchers wishing to confirm or extend our data can contact these people through the author. All of us owe them an immense debt of gratitude for their generous cooperation.

From a survey of the literature, the clinical study of our own cases and laboratory findings, we present the thesis that a process, most usefully viewed as the "rise of the kundalini" is a reality, is much to be desired, and can be described as an evolutionary process taking place in the human nervous system.

It is interesting to note that our thesis is consistent with the observations of Gopi Krishna (1973, 1975), from his personal experience with the rising of his own kundalini. He says:

A new center—presently dormant in the average man and woman— has to be activated and a more powerful stream of psychic energy must rise into the head from the base of the spine to enable human consciousness to transcend the normal limits. This is the final phase of the present evolutionary impulse in man. The cerebrospinal system of man has to undergo a radical change, enabling consciousness to transcend the normal limits. This is the final phase of the present evolutionary impulse in man. The cerebrospinal system of man has to undergo a radical change, enabling consciousness to attain a dimension which transcends the limits of the highest intellect. Here reason yields to intuition and Revelation appears to guide the steps of humankind . . .

The living substance which, in an altered form, is responsible for causing this aesthetic revolution in the brain is entirely beyond our scrutiny and will remain so for a long time to come.

We shall begin our presentation by discussing the special significance of the rebirth process today and the problem of objectivity in the description of spiritual states. Then we shall present the kundalini concept from yoga tradition as the classical rebirth model most widely applicable, and most easily amenable, to physiological interpretation. But certain differences between the classical kundalini concept and our own cases will lead us to propose a variation, the *physio*-kundalini model, to account for our observations.

Our data consist of published reports from diverse cultures and many cases of our own. From these we shall summarize the characteristic signs and symptoms of the rebirth process, designating these the physio-kundalini complex. We derive this concept from a model recently proposed by Itzhak Bentov to explain the effects of kundalini. His is the first theory of the kundalini phenomenon subject to experimental verification. The significance of Bentov's work will be

4

discussed, and his paper is included here in the Appendix.

We consider how our findings relate to the classical yogic description of kundalini action. Then, in our discussion of diagnosis, we show that it is possible to recognize the physio-kundalini process and distinguish it from psychosis, even when these two conditions have temporarily merged in a particular individual. This distinction will help make it possible for clinicians to avoid the mistakes that have often been made in the past.

People undergoing the rebirth process often need special help. We shall consider what forms of help are advisable, and which are not. Finally, we shall suggest an approach for coping with the problems and opportunities generated by the rebirth phenomenon in society as a whole. Here we may be guided by the precedent of Meher Baba's work with *Masts*, so a second Appendix has been added on this subject. But why is rebirth possible at all? A third Appendix, "Sensitivity in the Human Organism", deals with this question. A fourth Appendix is for the use of medical specialists, and the final Appendix for clinicians.

Study in this area is timely—indeed it is urgent. The new preoccupation with spiritual and occult practices, especially among the young, holds both great promise and great danger. It is essential that we quickly arrive at a deeper understanding of this field.

THE SIGNIFICANCE OF
THE REBIRTH PROCESS

Gopi Krishna (1971) said that:

This mechanism, known as Kundalini, is the real cause of all genuine spiritual and psychic phenomena, the biological basis of evolution and development of personality, the secret origin of all esoteric and occult doctrines, the master key to the unsolved mystery of creation, the inexhaustible source of philosophy, art and science, and the fountainhead of all religious faiths, past, present and future.

Over forty years ago, in a seminar on kundalini, C. G. Jung (1932, 1975) and his colleagues observed that the rising of this force had rarely, if ever, been seen in the West. They suggested that it would take a thousand years for the kundalini to be set in motion by depth analysis.

However remote Jung considered the possibility of the rise of the kundalini in his time, he certainly had a clear grasp of its psychological significance. He tells of a medieval monk who took a fantasy journey into a wild, unknown forest where he lost his way. On trying to return he found his path barred by a fierce dragon. Jung says that this beast is the symbol of the kundalini, the force that, in psychological terms, makes a person go on his or her greatest adventures. When the going gets rough, one then recants, "Oh, damn, why did I ever try such a thing"; knowing that in turning back, the spirit of divine adventure will go out of life, and life will lose its flavor.

Jung (1975) says, "When you succeed in awakening the kundalini, so that it starts to move out of its mere potentiality, you necessarily start a world which is totally different from our world. It is a world of eternity."

He goes on to refer to the kundalini as an impersonal force. He says that if you claim it as your own creation you do so at your

6

peril. The price is ego inflation, false superiority, obnoxiousness, or madness. It is an autonomous process arising out of the unconscious that seems to use you as its vehicle.

Although this rebirth process was rare in 1932 when Jung wrote of it, it now occurs regularly, with and without training, as is shown by the growing number of cases in the files of the Kundalini Research Foundation in New York, and by our own increasing number of authenticated cases.

There is now much greater interest in this subject in the West, as can be seen by the rapid expansion of all sorts of mind training, new therapies, meditative practices, and psychic pursuits. Thousands of people are now engaged in or interested in such activities.

Even recently the great increase in the use of hallucinogenic drugs can be seen as a determined, if dangerous and misguided, urge in the direction of things of the spirit.

The marked increase in the number of individuals undergoing the rebirth transformation may be a reflection of a similar transformation taking place at a sociocultural level in society as a whole. Jung (1964) pointed out that a time of dissociation, such as prevailed during the Roman Empire and which prevails again in our own era, is simultaneously an age of death and rebirth: "When one principle reaches the height of its power, the counter principle stirring within, contains in its darkness the germ of a new light."

Gopi Krishna (1975) says:

There is a rebellion against the existing order, because the brain has reached a state of development where the riddle of existence looms larger in front than it did before. This is the reason why millions of young men and women in Europe and America are eagerly on the search for masters and effective methods of self-awareness.

. . . at a certain critical state in the development of the human mind the unanswered "Riddle of Life" attains an urgency which no treasure of the earth can counteract. This is the state of mind of millions of disillusioned young people of the world today. Modern psychology is absolutely dead to a most powerful impulse in the psychic make-up of man that has always been in evidence from the very dawn of civilization to this day.

7

When thwarted in its mission, the impulse can lead to social and political unrest...craving for drugs, promiscuity or other social evils and even to violence.

He then quotes an American physician, Dr. Treffert, director of a medical center in Wisconsin, who says:

... about 30 Americans under 21 years of age commit suicide every day, indicating a three-fold increase in the rate of suicide among American youth over the past decade. Also more than half the patients admitted to mental hospitals in the United States are young people ... the main cause of the increase in the number of suicides and mental disorders among the youth is the increasing hollowness and senselessness of life of the society and the younger generation's distaste for profit.

Pressures arising from the underlying shift in society place a demand on religious leaders and consciousness researchers to provide environments and methods for the rapid and safe development of the inner potentials of the increasing number of seekers.

THE PROBLEM OF OBJECTIVITY

In personal accounts of the rising of kundalini, there is an endless array of emotions, strange thoughts, and visions, but descriptions of physical signs and symptoms or *actual sensations* are rare. Allusions to vague subjectively perceived force fields and energy states are now common in descriptions of meditative experiences. Jung (1975) referred to the adherence to traditional models as a dogmatism that sprang from a long tradition of passing down principles from teacher to student. We see this commonly in the descriptions of kundalini experience in yogic schools.

While this is apparent from studying the Eastern writings, it is also true that in the West we have not clarified the different states of psyche and soma in accounts of transcendental experience. For example, William James (1929) saw the great German mystic, Suso, as a suffering ascetic incapable of turning his torments into religious ecstacy. On the other hand, the Jung group thought Suso had experienced awakened kundalini. These two views reflect the different interests that James and Jung brought to their study of Suso. James emphasized the ecstatic, and Jung was concerned with the relationship between individuation and kundalini.

However, Western science is now making objective laboratory measurements of changes accompanying spiritual phenomena as well as encouraging more open and direct accounts of personal experience. Perhaps this has been the stimulus for the East to do likewise. Some recent accounts are rich with valuable information, and we can expect many more in the near future. Descriptions of this kind transcend personal and cultural differences to reveal the essential similarity of the phenomena concerned.

The signs and symptoms usually described, such as alterations in emotions and thought processes, visions and voices, appear to

9

be largely personally determined. But the sensations such as itching, fluttering, tingling, heat and cold, perceptions of inner lights and sounds, and the occurence of contortions and spasms appear to be quite universal. It is this universality that leads us to postulate that all spiritual practices are activating the same basic process, and that this process has a definite physiological basis that gives rise to these specific bodily symptoms.

On the other hand, the emotional correlates of this process are also important. It is these, and the changed thinking that accompanies them, that result in this process frequently being mistaken for mental illness. It is also these aspects that ultimately provide the personal meaning of the transformation for the people who experience it.

We realize that we cannot present, in all their rich experiential detail, the broad spectrum of personal experiences these people have undergone; the intricacies of their feeling and thought processes, their ecstasies, and their desperate confusions. The compelling quality of these experiences overshadow the physiological details, so that the person tends to ignore subtle changes in his or her physical state. These vary so widely that it seems as if they have nothing in common. This is why we will limit ourselves to a focus on the physiological parameters that we can relate to Bentov's model.

KUNDALINI AS A MODEL
FOR THE REBIRTH PROCESS

Every spiritual tradition that is concerned with the rebirth process has its own model. Most of these are descriptions that stress the subjective side of the experience, either treating the objective signs as incidental or ignoring them. Thus, these accounts, however valid they may be on their own terms, are not helpful in making objective comparisons of different traditions. When it comes to physiological interpretations, most of these models have little relevance.

An exception is the kundalini model from yoga. Kundalini is seen as an energy that usually resides asleep at the base of the spine. When this energy is awakened, it rises slowly up the spinal canal to the top of the head. This may mark the beginning of a process of enlightenment.

In its rise, kundalini causes the central nervous system to throw off stress. The stress points will usually cause pain during meditation. When kundalini encounters these stress points or blocks, it begins to act on its own volition, engaging in a self-directed, self-limited process of spreading out through the entire physio-psychological system to remove these blocks. Once a block is removed, kundalini flows freely through that point and continues its upward journey until the next stress area is encountered. Further, the kundalini energy diffuses in this journey, so that it may be operating on several levels at once, removing several different blocks. When the course is completed, the energy all becomes focused again at the top of the head. The difference between this final state and the initial state is not simply that kundalini is focused in a different place, but that in the meantime it has passed through every part of the organism, removing blocks and awakening consciousness there. Thus, the entire process of kundalini action can be seen as one of purification or balancing.

Just as an electric current produces light when it passes through a thin tungsten filament, but not when it passes through a thick copper wire, because the filament offers appreciable resistance while the wire does not, so also does the kundalini cause the most sensation when it enters an area of mind or body that is blocked. But the heat generated by the friction of kundalini against this resistance soon burns out the block, and then the sensation ceases. Similarly, just as an intense flow of water through a small rubber hose will cause the hose to whip about violently, while the same flow through a fire-hose would scarcely be noticed, so also does the flow of kundalini through obstructed channels within the body or mind cause motions of those areas until the obstructions have been washed out and the channels widened. (The terms "channel", "widen", "blocks", and so on must be taken metaphorically. They may not refer to actual physical structures, dimensions and processes, but are only useful analogies for understanding this model of kundalini action. The actual process is undoubtedly much more subtle and complex.)

The spontaneous movements, shifting body sensations, and other phenomena reported in our cross-cultural survey and in our own cases, can easily be interpreted as manifestations of kundalini action. Furthermore, Bentov has recently proposed a physiological model for kundalini that accounts for much of what we have reported and observed. His study is evaluated in terms of our results later. Because of the objective orientation of his kundalini model, its universal applicability, and its susceptibility to physiological interpretation, we shall adopt it as the basis for our discussions.

However, there are differences between our own observations and the classical kundalini concept. Most notably, we observe, and several traditions report, that the energy or sensation rises up the feet and legs, the body, back and spine to the head, but then passes down over the face, and through the throat, finally terminating in the abdomen. This is entirely in accord with predictions from Bentov's

12

model, but somewhat at variance with the reports of Muktananda, Gopi Krishna and classic yoga scriptures.

Therefore we propose the term physio-kundalini to refer to those aspects of kundalini awakening, both physiological and psychological, which can be accounted for by a purely physiological mechanism. We shall refer to the physio-kundalini process, the physio-kundalini cycle, the physio-kundalini mechanism, and the physio-kundalini complex. Bentov's model describes such physiological changes that require no super-normal forces.

The slow progression of energy sensation up through the body, then down the throat, accompanied by a variety of movements, sensations, and mental disturbances that terminate when this traveling stimulus reaches its culmination in the abdomen is so characteristic, that we shall call it the *physio-kundalini cycle*. When the energy encounters a resistance, then overcomes it and purifies the system of that block, we shall say that the location of that block has been opened. The throat-opening is one typical example. This gives us a terminology linked to the kundalini concept, suited to the level of our observations and amenable to physiological interpretation. At the same time, it preserves the full integrity of the classical meaning of kundalini without committing us to a belief that this mystical concept is accurate or corresponds to anything objectively real.

Body consciousness
→ transcendence

CROSS-CULTURAL
ASPECTS OF KUNDALINI

In Africa

Katz (1973) writes of the !Kung people of the Kalahari Desert in Northwest Botswana, Africa, who dance for many hours to "heat" up the *n/um* so that the *!kia* state can be attained. He notes that n/um is analogous to the kundalini state. !Kia is the state of transcendence. It is more than a peak experience of going beyond the ordinary self; !kia is like Satori, participation in eternity. Education for transcendence teaches the adept the way to stir up the n/um and how the threshold of fear can be crossed into the !kia state. The n/um is said to reside in the pit of the stomach. As it warms up, it rises from the base of the spine to the skull where then !kia occurs.

According to the report of a tribesman:

> You dance, dance, dance, dance. Then n/um lifts you in your belly and lifts you in your back, and then you start to shiver. N/um makes you tremble; it's hot. Your eyes are open but you don't look around; you hold your eyes still and look straight ahead. But when you get into !kia, you're looking around because you see everything, because you see what's troubling everybody . . . Rapid shallow breathing, that's what draws n/um up . . . then n/um enters every part of your body, right to the tip of your feet and even your hair.

Another says:

> In your backbone you feel a pointed something, and it works its way up. Then the base of your spine is tingling, tingling, tingling, tingling, tingling, tingling, tingling . . . and then it makes your thoughts nothing in your head.

The !kia is an intense emotional state. At its height the n/um master practices extraordinary activities such as curing the sick, handling and walking on fire; a master has X-ray vision and may see over great distances, but does not even attempt such activities in his ordinary state.

14

One master said that when he is in the !kia state, "I can really become myself again", implying that these unusual activities are the natural right of a person.

Transcending himself, a master is able to contact the supernatural realm and combat the ghosts that cause illness. The struggle with the ghosts is at the heart of the n/um master's art, skill, and power. Just as at the moment of transcendence fear of dying is overcome so that rebirth may occur, so at the moment of healing the battle with sickness is won.

The sole criterion for determining who becomes a n/um master is the process itself. Every person who experiences n/um and is able to !kia is automatically a n/um master. The more emotional you are and the richer your fantasy life the more apt you are to !kia (transcend). Over half the tribe members can attain this state and !kia seems to run in families.

!kia is painful, fearful, and unpredictable each time it occurs. As in many close Guru relationships the idea is that the teacher puts n/um into the student. The Guru also controls the process so that the excessive fear does not prevent the occurrence of !kia. Though originally from the gods, n/um now passes regularly from person to person.

Katz points out that the !Kung seek !kia not only for their own personal enrichment, but to help others. Nor is it cultivated as a long term condition. A tribe member must soon return to an ordinary state and the usual responsibilities. An extended !kia is not seen as a state of grace but as a mistake. !kia is for entering the religious dimension, receiving its nourishment, sharing it in healing, and then to return and live this truth with one's fellows.

Katz says that there are few teachers among us in the West who can help others toward transcendence, being relatively incomplete beings ourselves. We are at a further disadvantage, operating as we do, without a context that exists culturally to support the idea of education for transcendence.

15

In the Christian Tradition

Saint Therese of Lisieux (1873-1897) is reported to have undergone sufferings similar to those we have observed (Rohrback, 1963). She was from a middle class French family with happily married parents and four sisters. When she was ten she became a student at a nearby Carmelite convent. A few months after she enrolled she began to have constant headaches. Three months later as she prepared for bed one evening, she began to shiver uncontrollably. These spells continued for a week and were uninfluenced by any treatment. She had no fever and once the shivering was over, it never returned.

A few weeks later she was stricken with a "strange melange of hallucinations, comas and convulsions". She appeared to be in delirium, crying out against unseen and terrifying creatures. She tossed violently in bed hitting her head on the bedboards as if some strange force were assailing her. These "convulsions", which sometimes resembled the actions of a gymnast, were occasionally so violent that she would be thrown out of bed. There were rotary or tumbling movements of her whole body of which she was incapable when she was well. For example, she would spring from her knees and stand on her head without using her hands.

Later, while at Mass, she had a more severe attack which terminated upon her praying earnestly. In all, this whole illness lasted less than two months. Later, two more incidents occurred; fainting and rigidity which lasted for only a few moments. Throughout all this, Therese said she never lost awareness, even during the "fainting", but that she had no control over her actions.

She was attended regularly by a competent physician who was unable to help her and frankly admitted to being confused by her symptoms. He was very firm in his statement that "it was not hysteria".

Heat Manifestations in Different Cultures

Heat is one of the more easily observed and measured manifestations that may accompany an active kundalini state. Two examples from the Sufi literature are worth noting (Bhavan, 1971).

Then the saint came to take a meal, and the girl was pouring water on his hands. She noticed that so intense was the fire of separation burning in him that immediately the water would fall on his hands it would pass into vapor.

By troth I see, as the physician tries to touch my hand, his hand is burnt and patches and swellings immediately appear on it. Such is the heat of the fire of separation. He alone knoweth my condition who hath endured such pain cheerfully when it fell to his lot.

Tony Agpaoa (1974), a Phillippine psychic surgeon who has received much notoriety, said that he learned to ignite fires by mental means as part of his training as a healer. Swami Muktananda (1975) said that this ability is part of the training in certain yogic disciplines. The widespread tradition of objective heat manifestation adds credence to similar manifestations in our own cases.

In recent times many instances of paranormal spontaneous combustion have been well documented. There are many cases in the literature. I will note one of these, and report my own experience. H. Andrade (1975) reports that many fires occurred spontaneously in a case he investigated and that some of them were witnessed by police officers.

I spent two years investigating a poltergeist case where fires broke out frequently (Morris, 1974). The situation was emotionally and religiously complicated. It involved a Jewish and a Catholic family with intermarriage between them. When a son was born to the young Jewish man and Catholic woman, the poltergeist activity started with the events centering around the baby, symbols of the marriage, and religious artifacts.

Soon the young man decided to convert to Catholicism. This, together with the poltergeist activity itself, threw the families into great turmoil. All the family members of four generations and several other people experienced the movement of objects, their disappearance, and spontaneous fires. The young couple suffered sensations of being struck, shaken, scratched, and choked. The girl's mother was struck and knocked unconscious one evening and had to be hospitalized.

There were a number of spontaneous fires witnessed by each family member and by several investigators. My first experience occurred one evening when the grandfather went into the bedroom to check on the baby and found the curtains ablaze. He and I both burned our hands slightly in putting the fire out. I was present when several other small fires broke out.

This is a possible example of how pent-up energy can express itself objectively at a distance. After the young man converted to Catholism, avidly invested his energy in the Church, and secured an official exorcism, the phenomena ceased.

In the Orient

In the Chinese Taoist tradition (Luk, 1972), after one has learned to achieve stillness of mind, hitherto dormant excellent qualities will manifest themselves. The vital principle, prana, now sufficiently accumulated in the lower belly, bursts out and begins to flow in the main psychic channels of the body causing involuntary movements. Also, eight physical sensations are produced: pain, itching, coldness, warmth, weightlessness, heaviness, roughness, and smoothness.

The vital element is hot, and not only spreads its warmth to parts of the body, but may even become bright and perceptible to the meditator. In exceptional meditators it causes illumination of a dark room perceptible to others. When the vital principle flows into obstructed psychic centers it is quite unpleasant, causing feelings of roughness, cramping and pain.

Luk reports Yin Shih Tsu as writing in 1914 that he felt heat

18

going from the base of his spine to the top of his head, then down over his face and throat to his stomach. His whole body turned and twisted and he saw a variety of internal lights. He had headaches and one time his head felt swollen. The upper part of his body seemed to stretch so that he felt ten feet tall. This is spoken of as the Great Body in Buddhist scriptures.

Yin Shih Tsu said that he did not feel all these things at one time but a few at different times in his meditative experiences. Sometimes the circulating heat felt more like vibrations following the described path. Once, for a period of six months, he experienced nightly involuntary yogic postures that occurred in an orderly sequence.

In the Korean Zen experience this same progression of sensation is reported. Seo (1974) said that the chi energy travels up the body, especially the back, then over the top of the head to the face, finally passing down through the throat to terminate in the abdomen.

Uroboros

In one modern esoteric school, Arica, the uroboros, or snake swallowing its tail is an exercise in which energy is seen to be generated in the lower abdomen directed by the breathing. On inhalation one focuses on the perineal area, first sensing, then directing the energy up the spine to the back of the head. Then it curves over the skull, and with the expired breath begins its downward path. It goes through the center of the head to the forehead where it splits at the eyes and goes down the sides of the nose and upper lip to meet at the chin. (A similar splitting occurs in the Korean Zen teaching and in the ancient Egyptian symbol of the eye of Osiris.) From the chin it continues down the front of the throat through the breastbone to end in the lower abdomen. The purpose of the exercise is to "see" a light in the head.

Some Classical Yoga Accounts

Swami Narayanananda (1960) reports on the experience of kundalini:

There is a burning up the back and over the whole body. Kundalini's entrance into *Sushumna* (the central spinal canal) occurs with pain in the back . . . One feels a creeping sensation from the toes and sometimes it shakes the whole body. The rising is felt like that of an ant creeping up slowly over the body towards the head. Its ascent is felt like the wiggling of a snake or a bird hopping from place to place.

The translator of Ramakrishna's biography, Nikkhilananda, describes the experience in strikingly similar words. In Joseph Campbell's (1974) book, *A Mythic Image*, we read on page 306:

Now there was in the last century a great Indian saint, Ramakrishna (1836-1886), who in the practices of this yoga was a veritable virtuso. "There are", he once told his devotees, "five kinds of samadhi;" five kinds, that is to say, of spiritual rapture.

In these samadhis one feels the sensation of the Spiritual Current to be like the movement of an ant, a fish, a monkey, a bird, or a serpent.

Sometimes the Spiritual Current rises through the spine, crawling like an ant. Sometimes, in samadhi, the soul swims joyfully in the ocean of divine ecstasy, like a fish. Sometimes, when I lie down on my side, I feel the Spiritual Current pushing me like a monkey and playing with me joyfully. I remain still. That Current, like a monkey, suddenly with one jump reaches the Sahasrar. That is why you see me jump up with a start. Sometimes, again, the Spiritual Current rises like a bird hopping from one branch to another. The place where it rests feels like fire . . . Sometimes the Spiritual Current moves up like a snake. Going in a zigzag way, at last it reaches the head and I go into samadhi. A man's spiritual consciousness is not awakened unless his Kundalini is aroused.

The great work by Swami Vishnu Tirtha (1962) builds an excellent bridge between the classicists and moderns in the yoga tradition. In one small volume this holy man categorizes the signs of an early awakening in a most personal and picturesque fashion. All of the different sense systems are covered as well as the motor and other manifestations also. The more intimate personal accounts of Gopi Krishna and Muktananda seem to spring naturally from his fresh approach.

Also in the kundalini yoga tradition, Swami Muktananda (1974) has recently published an autobiography rich in description of sensations, involuntary movements, flows of energy through the body, unusual breathing patterns, inner lights and sounds, formed visions and voices, and many other extraordinary experiences.

He says, "My body was heated up and my head became heavy . . . the spinal base was rent with pain."

He assumed involuntary yogic positions and his body became stiff as a board. He smelled perfumes during meditation, and he tasted nectar. He heard sounds of ocean surf, thunder, brook murmurs, the crackle of fire, drums, conch shell sounds, bells, and bird calls.

In describing one important process he writes, "My eyes gradually rolled up and became centered . . . Instead of seeing separately, . . . they saw as one."

The entire progression, which lasted several years, finally culminated when, he says, he passed beyond all such experiences to become permanently established in the absolute equanimity of the transcendental state.

From a clinical standpoint it is important to note that in the early stages of his kundalini awakening he was often confused and fearful, having no control over his wild body movements, awkward postures, or dazzling lights he saw in his head. At times he believed he was going insane. It is easy to imagine the diagnosis if he had approached a psychiatrist instead of his Guru for help. And yet now these experiences have spontaneously culminated in a state in which he functions very well and is able to help many who come to him.

Another living practitioner of kundalini yoga, Gopi Krishna (1971), has also recently published an autobiography containing similar kinds of observations. This book includes a psychological commentary by James Hillman comparing Krishna's kundalini experience with the Jungian model of psychosis.

Krishna had meditated for many years working largely without a teacher. He had no sort of religious experiences until 1937 when he was thirty-four years old. He writes of this experience:

I distinctly felt an incomparable blissful sensation in all my nerves moving from the tips of fingers and toes and other parts of the trunk and limbs towards the spine, where, concentrated and intensified, it mounted upwards with a still more exquisitely pleasant feeling to pour into the upper region of the brain.

This sensation left when he paid attention to it, but when he ignored it, it flowed up with increased intensity. Suddenly with a roar like that of a waterfall he felt a stream of liquid light entering his brain through the spinal cord. His body then began to rock and he was enclosed in a halo of light, became one with his surroundings, and had feelings of bliss.

Following this, he had great fear, weakness, and indifference to people. His mouth tasted bitter, he felt terror, and he was often very hot. He noted a reddish glow around himself in the dark. There was a sensation like hot pins throughout his body, his throat felt scorched, and at times he had severe back pains. He felt that his kundalini was operating in the wrong manner and that he might die.

Once he had the Great Body experience, "I felt as if I were looking at the world from a higher elevation than that from which I saw it before."

He had psychic experiences as a child but was agnostic as a young man. He nonetheless, took yoga meditation which ultimately led to his kundalini experience. After the beginning of his awakening he was at the mercy of the kundalini process. It took many years before he attained a state of equanimity. This was followed by a gradual development of extraordinary mental gifts, emotional tranquility, and creative productivity.

An American Case

The last example in this series of published accounts is an American writer and Zen meditator whose "enlightenment" was verified by the famous Zen Master, Yasutani Roshi. I know this woman personally, but place her in this section because her account is in print.

Flora Courtois (1970) is a fifty-nine year old writer, who started her search many years ago when she began to question her teachers, and have doubts no one could help her with. Her first contact with an experience of "the deepest truth" came during a semi-conscious state following a general anesthetic. After spontaneous experiences in which she fused with nature, she became preoccupied with how visual perception occurs. When she wrote of her complex observations, a teacher thought she was mentally disturbed and sent her to a psychiatrist. This led to a short hospitalization which upset her greatly. She was so depressed over being misunderstood that she considered suicide. However, her suicidal thoughts ended one day when, "the focus of my sight seemed to have changed; it had sharpened to an infinitely small point which moved ceaselessly in paths totally free of the old accustomed ones as if flowing from a new source."

She then went into an ecstatic state that lasted for many days. Although she was immersed in ecstasy, it in no way interfered with her daily activities. Since then she has had a productive and happy life.

This case is of special interest because of the near tragedy resulting from the authorities' misunderstanding of her religious experience. It is of further interest because Courtois did not have many of the symptoms we find in other cases. Her adolescent experiences alone would lead one to anticipate more kundalini symptoms as she developed. But in 1967, when she began Zen meditation, which, in a person so sensitive in adolescence would be expected to bring on more symptoms, she had, instead, only one remarkable experience.

She was sitting in the meditation hall when she saw a bright light that was so real to her she believed the electric lights had actually been turned on. Although she realized she was still in relative darkness, she continued to see brightness for several minutes.

It may be that there is some constitutional difference between people who tend to have visionary experiences and those who tend toward kundalini. A third category includes persons who have predominantly psychic experiences, as opposed to visionary or kundalini experiences. We consider Courtois' experience, like those reported by Bucke (1970) and James (1929), to be visionary, while kundalini includes all visionary and psychic experiences, as well as its own characteristic features of the physio-kundalini complex.

It may also be that the Zen method discourages the experience of the rise of kundalini by its open-eye meditation, which encourages the meditator to flow with the external, as well as with the internal world. It also recommends that psychic experiences and unusual sensations be acknowledged and relinquished on the path to Satori.

Zen seems to attract intellectual and physical types. The Tibetan and Hindu traditions, with their rich and colorful symbols and rituals, appeal to emotional types. In addition, the path of devotion, so common in yoga, has a natural attraction for the emotional type of person.

Perhaps several of these factors played a role in the experiences of Flora Courtois.

CASE HISTORIES OF KUNDALINI EXPERIENCES

This section presents 13 people, 11 of whom I have personally interviewed, and 2 that were interviewed by a colleague. One of these two I also saw briefly. Some of these people were referred to me for their physical or psychological problems, or difficulties in meditation. Others, I sought out after hearing of their unusual experiences. Most of them have become personal friends and have shared their experiences with me in great depth over the past two years.

The first four cases are used to illustrate what we believe to be the most typical pattern of physio-kundalini. The next three show the remarkable heat manifestations that sometimes occur. The two cases that follow are "healers" in whom early physio-kundalini has occurred with subsequent increase in their effectiveness in their work. The next three cases are people who had life problems, internal resistances, or neurotic traits that complicated their physio-kundalini. The last case is included because it shows a sudden kundalini arising upon contact with a Guru.

Artist   Now a 48 year old woman artist, she started Transcendental Meditation, and after about 5 years began to experience occasional tingling in her arms and heat in the hands. She did not sleep for days, with energy surging through her whole body, and had several dreams of having her consciousness separated from her body. A continuous loud sound had appeared inside her head. Soon there were cramps in her big toes, followed by vibratory feelings in her legs. Overnight, her big toe nails darkened, as if hit by a hammer, and eventually partially separated from the flesh. The tissues in her legs felt torn through by vibratory sensations. The vibrations spread to her lower back and swept over her body from lower back up to her head, forming a sensation of a band around the head, just above the eyebrows. Then her head started to move spontaneously. Later her body moved sinuously and her tongue pressed to the roof of her mouth. Then she sensed a strong sound of "om" there. The tinglings spread back of her neck and head, over the head to her forehead and face. Both nostrils were stimulated, causing a feeling of elongation of the nose. The tinglings then spread down her face. At times her eyes seemed to move separately, and the pupils felt like holes that bored into her head and met in the center. Then she felt a tremendous head pressure and a brilliant light, followed by bliss and laughter. The tinglings spread further down to her upper lip, chin, and mouth. About this time there were dreams of heavenly music. Then the sensations went to her throat, chest and abdomen, and eventually she felt as if there was a closing of the circuit in the shape of an egg; up through the spine, down through the front of the body. As it developed, the circuit activated particular chakras on its way; starting in the lower abdomen, then the navel, the solar plexus, the heart, then the head centers. The last to be activated was the throat. After that there was a continuous feeling of energy pouring into the body through the navel area. This feeling stopped after the circuit was completed. The whole experience had strong sexual overtones. The greater part of this activity occurred over several months. In the last two years there has been only occasional activity, mostly during meditation, or when she is relaxed in bed.

During the experience there was spontaneous yogic breathing (faint and controlled). Eventually there developed head pressures, which centered around the back of the head, the top and the forehead. These pressures would become especially severe during reading, resulting in discomfort around eyes and a pulsing sensation at the top of the head.

The loud sound inside the head eventually disappeared. Throughout the experience she understood that she was undergoing the rising of kundalini, because she had read about it before. Therefore, she felt relaxed about it and just allowed things to happen. However, she became emotionally perturbed, and had difficulty in integrating these experiences with her daily activities.

Since the inflow of energy prevented normal sleep for months and continued during the day as well, work became inefficient, and she felt as if she was completely detached and was witnessing her own activities. Eventually, she brought the situation under control. The general effect was a greater emotional stability and elimination of tension, along with a greatly enhanced intuitive insight.

Scientist   A male scientist, now 53 years old, started Transcendental Meditation in 1967. Within 5 years he began to have gross thrashing body movements during meditation and at night in bed. After a few weeks these subsided. Months later, on going to bed, he felt tingling in his lower legs, followed by cramping in his big toes. The cramping extended to other muscles and gradually faded. The tingling rose to his lower back and he "saw" a reddish light there. The light became like a rod which he felt and saw being pushed up his spine. Then it extended forward to the umbilical area with many tingling, vibrating sensations. Step by step, it proceeded up the spine to the level of his heart and then extended forward to stimulate the cardiac plexus. When it reached his head, he "saw" floods of white light, as if his skull were lit up from inside. Then the light seemed to spout out the top of his head as a solid beam. Some time later he felt a vibration in his right wrist, arm, and also in his left leg. As soon as he attended to these sensations, they disappeared. Then the feeling of currents running through his shoulders and arms as "waves of current" occurring three or four per second, later increasing to seven and more per second. At one time, when he focused on the center in his head, violent and uncontrollable spasms occurred.

At various times, during all of this activity, he was aware of sounds in his head, mostly of high-pitched whistling and hissing.

At other times, he heard flute-like musical tones. Very frequently there were feelings of peace and bliss.

His sleep began to be disturbed by automatic movements of his body. Sometimes he would awaken to find himself doing spon--taneous yogic breathing and assuming various hatha yoga positions. After several nights of this, the tingling went to his forehead, nostrils, cheeks, mouth, and chin. During this process he had many ecstatic feelings and sexual stimulation when the activity centered in the pelvic area. Then all this ceased and returned from time to time when he relaxed at night in bed. He could shut these off by turning on his side.

About a year later, pressures developed in his head at night and started moving downward. Simultaneously, a tingling sensation started moving up from the stomach. He saw all this happening to him as if from a distance. The two stimuli met at his throat. He felt as if a hole appeared in his throat at the point where they met. From this hole all manner of purely spontaneous sounds were emitted. He had little control over these. About 6 months later the stimulus moved down from his throat to the abdomen, where it remained for a few months. Then they moved further down into the pelvis.

This scientist had an inherently sensitive nervous system, but his awareness that he was going through the rise of kundalini and his knowledge of what to expect, together with the stabilizing effect of a meditative discipline, made him less susceptible to the disorganizing aspects of kundalini. He realized that the difficulties that he did have were the result of over strenuous meditative prac-tice, and so he developed no anxieties during the process.

Actress A 29 year old actress had many psychic experiences in childhood. As an adolescent she suffered from recurring mi-graine headaches, mental disorganization, and impulsive disruptive behavior. She received psychotherapy for these symptoms for several years, was diagnosed schizophrenic, but was never hospitalized. When she was twenty-four she began to meditate using various techniques.

About a year later, her headaches became worse. Then, within a few weeks her head pains, mental disorganization, and disruptive behavior suddenly ceased. Within a year tinglings began in her legs, then spread to her arms and chest. After a few weeks they extended to her neck and the back of her head, and soon to her forehead. They were more noticeable during meditation. At intervals her entire body, but especially her hands became very hot. Also during meditation, she was troubled by swaying and jerking of her body, and by anxiety.

She came to our attention because of the severity of her anxiety and the violence of the spontaneous body movements during meditation. We advised her to discontinue her self-styled meditation and take up some established meditative practice. Until this was possible, we suggested that she temporarily decrease her sensitivity to the process by discontinuing her periodic fasting and strict vegetarian diet. When she was able to begin supervised meditation with Transcendental Meditation techniques, all disturbing symptoms soon ceased.

Sometime later the physio-kundalini cycle began again. During one long meditation, she became aware of her throat in a new way. She felt as if her head had become separated and floated above her body; her throat started making sounds on its own, and she became aware of a separate observer-self. Most of her kundalini symptoms ceased after this experience; a typical "throat-opening".

Since then her meditations have been quiet and peaceful for the first time in years. She finds her productivity and contentment have greatly increased. She is now making a documentary film, a project she had long wanted to carry out.

We postulate that many psychotic-like aspects of her personality arose due to her failure to find a usable outlet for her psychic energies of a kind suitable to her nature.

Pertinent to the matter of psychic talent and its use is the experience of Matthew Manning (1975), an outstanding 20-year-

29

old British psychic, who was plagued by poltergeist phenomena from an early age. These persisted until one day he found that he could do automatic writing. Soon he found that he could paint in the style of several great painters, completing a work in ten to twenty minutes. This then turned out to be his most fruitful channel of expression. Once the bulk of his energy could be thus expressed, the poltergeist activity ceased.

It may be that in child geniuses (whose works are of the more usual kind, such as music, or graphic art) easy access to this one mode of expression stabilizes them early in life. The culture, church, and family, all support such an acceptable pursuit, and there are few conflicts. Child psychics may have it difficult from the start because of the disturbing and disruptive nature of their genius. Also, true spirituality, rarely if ever, emerges as early as these other talents. Even Jesus, Buddha, and Ramana Maharshi did not come into their spiritual genius until puberty or later.

There seems to be something special about creativity that manifests as great art: such as the products of a great writer, musician, or poet, the pictures and sculpture of an artist, or the choreography and dance of one who works primarily with the body. There is something so concrete about these artistic creations, that they seem to tie their creators to the world, not favoring the development of kundalini-type nervous system changes. Or possibly, there are fewer conflicts and blocks in the nervous system when genius is narrowly channeled, and so the nervous system change may occur without the physical results we know as kundalini. Also, these kinds of geniuses seem to be either psychic or visionary; in neither of these does kundalini seem to express itself in the classical manner. It may be that geniuses whose works are so concrete and familiar, thereby find an acceptance that leaves them relatively free from inner doubts as to their own productions. At least we suggest that their direct spiritual contacts of a non-physical nature must arise from a less gross, more subtly functioning area of the nervous system than does the kundalini. Finally, we suggest that the central nervous system must be relatively mature for the physio-kundalini process to occur at all.

Psychologist   In 1973 a 41 year old woman psychologist, who had been engaged in various intensive group and meditative disciplines for years, noted the onset of heat in her head and chest with tingling over her body and head while meditating. Soon, when she experienced these sensations, her tongue would move around of its own accord inside and outside her mouth. Whenever her tongue touched her soft palate she would have orgasmic waves through her body.

She was cold much of the time, though the coldness was mixed with heat. She felt shaped like an egg and her whole being felt unified. Vibrations moved in her pelvis and then up her back and to the neck. Her chest felt soft and open. She heard brilliant bird songs inside her head and felt a tingling in her throat. Once, three years earlier, she had felt like a giant heart while meditating. There was a prickly itching heat all over her body, but she was not troubled because she believed that these sensations indicated successful and centered meditations and a flow between herself and others. She assumed that she was having the rise of the kundalini which she believed to be dangerous unless the "higher mind" was in control.

A few months after this onset, during meditations, she felt as if she were two feet taller than her normal self and as if her eyes were looking out from above her head. At this time she was sure that she knew what people were thinking and many of her impressions were confirmed.

Soon after this, her feet began to hurt and headaches started. The headaches were worse when she attempted to control them. She noted that they came when she tried to control the rush of energy passing through her body. Massage helped the pain in her feet, but it was, nevertheless, so severe that she was unable to drive and walked with difficulty. It was hard for her to talk with people She ate very little, her sleep was fitful, and she had some nausea.

31

Many times she questioned the reality of her experiences, and wondered if she were going crazy.

She felt heat on one side of her back, and was convinced that unless it spread to both sides she would be in danger. Once she succeeded in spreading it this crisis passed.

Then a tingling started to move from her pelvis up her back and to her neck. She began to see light inside her head. She was amazed to find that she could see this light all the way down her spine as well. The energy and tingling moved over her forehead and became focused under her chin. She felt as if there were a hole in the top of her head. Sleep was very difficult, and for the next six weeks meditation was the only thing that helped her. She felt that if she did not meditate, the heat flowing in her body would grow so intense as to damage her. Other people could feel excessive heat when they touched her lower back.

Although she felt insane at times, she could differentiate her state from the emotional and mental breakdown of schizophrenia because of her psychological training. She felt it was necessary to avoid psychiatric help during her trouble because of the danger of being labeled and treated as insane. When her symptoms were more than she could bear alone, she worked with various meditation teachers.

A few months ago she began to have rippling and shaking of her body, and felt as though she was being cleansed and balanced. Shortly afterwards she felt a prickling in her cheeks and under her chin. Then all the unpleasantness ceased and she has had no more difficulty. She had gone through this much of the physio-kundalini cycle within a year, and now is continuing her meditation without any difficulty.

Now she is running a successful growth center where one of her major focuses is to help others who are troubled with difficulties in the kundalini process.

Her many distressing physical problems were probably due to

residual blocks and unresolved conflicts which were locked into her body. These probably would not have caused her any significant emotional or physical problems had her kundalini remained inactive.

Three Cases With Heat Manifestations

Librarian   A 44 year old woman librarian had been a meditator in her own style for many years. One day in 1968 she lost awareness while meditating with her hands on a table. She awoke to find charred marks that deeply marred the table and corresponded to her hand prints.

She had the table refinished too soon for me to examine it. No heat manifestations of this kind ever happened again. Because she did not show a regular progression of symptoms, we regarded her as a possible case of arrest of the physio-kundalini process.

In 1969 she acquired a psychic guide which she found very useful in her daily life. In 1972 she became involved in studying the dreams and drawings of children, and she completed an impressive manuscript on this work. Since this involvement, the intervention of her guide has ceased.

At this writing, she reports the development of a sort of stigmata. This is a vertical oval which appears in the center of her forehead at intervals of several months. It was about one inch by half an inch, noticeably red, and does not stand above the skin level. It has only happened twice. Each time she quickly did her best to hide it with cosmetics, just as she immediately got the table refinished when the charred hand prints occurred.

Her tendencies were to move along psychic paths. Her long studies of Jung may have led her to the faculty she developed with inner dialogue as seen in the episodes of her conversations with her psychic guide.

Professor   A middle-aged male professor, who had had many psychic experiences as a child, awoke from a nap in 1963, to find a 3-inch blister on his thigh where his hand had been resting. This extraordinary experience stimulated his interest in the power of the mind. Within 2 years he was meditating regularly, but without a teacher. In 1967, he began formal Zen meditation.

A few months later during a sitting, he became engulfed by a bright golden light that lasted several minutes. A few weeks later this occurred again.

During many sittings he noticed the movement of prickling and itching sensations up the inside of his legs to his groin, on his arms and chest, up his back and over his head to his brows. Then it moved to his cheeks, the outside of his nostrils, and sometimes to his chin. At the present time his meditations are characterized by tingling and itching in his throat. We would describe this as a typical physio-kundalini cycle that is currently at the stage of the throat-opening.

This man's course can be contrasted to that of the librarian, where the beginnings were similar, but he chose to pursue a regular traditional form of meditation with others as well as alone. We have the impression that such regularity and practice seems to favor a steady progression of what we have called the physio-kundalini cycle as occurred in his case. The less disciplined, psychically oriented forms of centering seem to favor their own sort of development with stress on trance states, entities, and like phenomena.

Writer   A 40 year old male writer had been meditating for 2 years when he began experiencing many subjective heat sensations. During one such episode he took his oral temperature (with an electronic thermometer): it was 101 degrees F, but fell within a minute or two to 99 degrees F. A short time later his hand temperature was 104 degrees F. He was not ill.

His earlier history is of interest. After he had been meditating for two years, he began experiencing spontaneous trance states. During these he received information psychically, some of which was confirmed. He came to our attention as a result of marital difficulties brought on by his trance states. We encouraged him to learn to enter a light trance state at will. His trance states then stopped. He is a productive writer and a successful wood sculptor.

The physical signs or manifestations of this man were similar to those of the preceeding two cases. His personality and interests tended more along the inner line of the librarian. He has made no connections to traditional Eastern methods of meditation. He did study briefly at one time several years ago with a curandero healer very similar to the man called Don Juan in the account by Castaneda (1968). He was more attracted by these powerful outer psychic manifestations than to the inner dialogue, and this may partially explain his being taken over in a rather autonomous manner by his trance states. Jung has repeatedly pointed out that if hidden inner drives are not somehow dealt with in dreams or through some form of inner dialogue, they will find expression in oblique autonomous overwhelming ways, such as in the trances that troubled this man.

Two Healers

Artist-Healer   A 27 year old male artist remembers his earliest psychic experiences as being lucid dreams in childhood. During one, he saw his double pick up the bed clothes, which had fallen off, and hand them to him. He was frightened by the vividness of this experience.

When he was 22, he began Transcendental Meditation, and had many insights and much tension release. Then he made such rapid progress in meditation without proper instruction that he started to have anxiety attacks while meditating. Once he had a vision of white light and lost consciousness. He experienced a flow of sensation just preceding this vision which started in his belly and went to his back,

35

neck, and the back of his head, where it burst into brilliant light. Then he felt heat in his head and belly. Hissing and roaring sounds developed during meditations. As the anxiety got worse, he shifted to Zen meditation where he found some relief. Soon after this, he had another white light vision much like the first one.

Two months later he went abroad with his family where he visited several psychic healers. He had psychic surgery for life long migraine headaches. This was about two years ago and he has had no recurrences. His family members were likewise healed of a number of chronic disorders. He was so impressed with what he saw, that he decided to return and film one of the healers. Just prior to leaving, he began to have precognitive visions. During the filming, he became so intrigued that he decided to study with one of the healers. He studied for two years, and found that he became more and more successful at healing, experiencing energy flows, and clairvoyantly sensing a person's malady.

He has recently returned to the United States where he is finding increasing success in his art work. He heals friends and acquaintances whenever the opportunity presents itself.

During this time he has continued and increased his meditation; with this, there has developed some tingling in his checks and sides of his nose. A return of the old anxiety soon subsided when several persons recovered from serious illnesses while working with him. He had been quite unsure that his recently acquired abilities, only contracted at the very end of his training period abroad, would be available to him here in this environment far removed from his teacher. This evidence reassured him and eased his anxiety.

Engineer-Healer   A 54 year old male former aeronautical engineer has been a healer and meditator for many years. In 1973 he suddenly began to have unusual body sensations. He felt pressure in his head, followed by a week of insomnia. Then the pressure changed to a vibratory sensation, and he felt heat inside his body. As the vibrations spread to his shoulders, chest, and down his legs, he felt as if his body would explode. When these sensations were strong, the back of his tongue would often blister. Waves of colored light poured through his body and head, becoming golden as it flowed. After three weeks of this, he felt washed clean, and found that he could control most of the sensations through meditation. He believes his ability as a healer has increased as a result of these experiences. My inquiries of those he has helped seem to confirm his impression.

These two healers illustrate extremes of self-discipline of a particular type. In the younger man, this was to apprentice himself to a mature healer with whom he worked for two years before realizing the results he sought. The older man likewise made his discipline a way of life but in a solitary setting where every night for five years he awoke early to meditate for two hours. He trained himself to sleep instantly at the end of these sessions. After this long practice he learned to separate his consciousness the moment he lay down. He practiced this for years before he had it under his control.

The training of these two was quite different. The first used an intuitive method in a setting that evoked his instincts to their full, while the other exercised a great deal of will and one pointed effort.

We saw another example of this sort of difference in approach recently in testing a professional psychic with magnetic stimulation of his right brain. We used the method Bentov describes in Appendix A. For some time following stimulation with a pulsating magnetic field to the right side of his head, he found that he could only visualize colors in the blue-green part of the spectrum, and that his word flow was impaired. The problem with language cleared in a few days, but the visualizations in full color took a week longer to return. Some stiffness in his neck, which also had its onset with the stimulation resolved at about the same time the color visualizing returned.

We believe that this man had been operating as a successful psychic from a mode in which his will was prominent. This probably favors continuing left brain dominance. His inherent sensitivity permitted him, when stimulated, to respond to a new kind of activity stirred up by the test. This new activity of his right brain then came into competition with the usual, well-controlled state in which the left brain was dominant. This may explain the initial left-sided symptoms (see p. 67). Thus the temporary state of confusion followed until his accustomed homeostasis was again estabished.

Three Cases With Complications

Secretary   A 28 year old woman secretary had been practicing Transcendental Meditation for two years. Early in 1975 she began having tingling and numbness in her lower legs. Soon stiffness in one leg began to interfere with walking. At this time she went to several doctors, including neurologists. When myelographic studies (spinal injection of radio-opaque oil with X-rays) were suggested, she refused. It occurred to her that her symptoms were worse after days in which she had been doing prolonged meditations, so she decided to seek advice about the effects of her meditative practice.

It looked likely that she was in the early stages of the physiokundalini cycle, and that the stress and worry about possible physical disease was increasing her difficulties. She had the wisdom to see that the nature of her symptoms suggested a process that was related to meditation.

We reassured her that her symptoms were part of a normal process in the nervous system that was proceeding too rapidly because of overdoing her meditations. Reassurance and temporary cessation of meditation, soon had her on the road to recovery. Later she resumed meditating in moderation. Her physio-kundalini cycle is now proceeding without incident.

Housewife   A 28 year old housewife had recently begun Transcendental Meditation. Soon she began to develop tingling and occasional stocking-type numbness in her left foot and leg. When subjected to the stress of her mother-in-law moving into the house with her and her husband, she started to get a stiff leg and developed a foot-drop. She went for medical help and a myelogram was done. Following this, all her symptoms increased. Then she was put on cortisone, and was told by her neurologist that she might never recover full use of her leg. Hearing this, she became severely depressed and nearly nonfunctional. At this time she came to our attention.

She had an extraordinarily sensitive nervous system, and was in the early stages of a physio-kundalini cycle. Her worry about the prognosis, and the effect of the cortisone increased her symptoms: pain and stiffness in her back and legs, and the paralysis already noted. Her therapy, and its successful outcome were the same as for the previous case.

Housewife A housewife in her mid fifties had the onset of a profound and disturbing process four years ago with a feeling that something was descending over her head,* followed by a fainting spell. These incidents recurred several times, but she was never groggy after regaining awareness as might be expected with a convulsive disorder. Physicians were unable to give her any relief.

One time she heard a voice saying inside her head, "Are you ready?" And later she heard internal music.

One day she was feeling well until late in the afternoon when she felt a pain developing at the base of her left big toe. This extended up the shin, was very painful, and she could feel the inside workings of her knee joint. The intermittent pain continued. She spent the next few days in bed where she spontaneously assumed many yogic asanas (positions). A few days later her body felt

---

* Roy (1974). His co-author Devi describes in almost identical words this experience which happened at her first meditation. This was soon followed by a remarkable and spontaneous kundalini experience.

worked on from the toes and up the back in segments. This process rose up her body and she had pain on both sides of her nose and waves of sensation up her neck and down her face. This was accompanied by intense heat in her back. She also had severe vise-like pressures around her head. During some of these flows of sensation she was forced to breathe in a sighing manner and there were occasionally torsional whipping movements of her head and neck. Once this energy came down into her head, and her scalp got cold while her fact got hot.

Over a period of about three years, she slowly became convinced that she had been selected by God to be born anew as an advanced human being. She had yielded to a tendency that Jung (1975) had warned against: that of claiming this force as her own ego creation, and as a result, falling into the trap of ego inflation and false superiority. Further, she became distrustful of those who heard her story but did not agree with her interpretations. She expected others to know exactly what she was speaking about and to accept all that she said without question. She has never done any regular meditation and is not interested in trying it. She had no interest in any help we had to offer.

SUDDEN KUNDALINI ARISING

A 33 year old male psychiatrist, a colleague of mine, and a member of our kundalini research team, has been meditating regularly for three years, and has served as a subject in our research with the magnetic stimulator. He was born with a spinal defect for which he had surgery that left him with chronic low back pain since his teens.

In December of 1975, he attended a weekend at the Muktananda ashram in Oakland, California. Upon being touched by Swami Muktananda, he went into deep meditation. Within ten minutes, he found that he could not speak, his mouth opened widely, and his tongue protruded. After a few minutes, he experienced a blissful calm and many inner visions, in which Muktananda appeared to him, and helped him experience a fusion with the Guru. A few minutes later he "saw" the interior of his abdomen, chest, and throat light up with a golden energy. At about this time, his lower back began to pain severely. As this happened, a white light in his head became more and more intense. Towards the end of this meditation, the back pain disappeared, and had not returned in the intervening four months.

Following this remarkable experience, his meditations at home have become very productive. Emotional problems and unfinished incidents seem to find solutions very rapidly and at great depth during his meditations.

In the middle of January, he developed a rash that formed a curved line from his lower back, crossed his spine twice, and veered off to the left shoulder. He questioned whether it might have a symbolic significance like a stigmata. At about this time, he noticed high-pitched noises and scratching sounds during meditation, which he had first experienced earlier after being stimulated many times over a period of months with our magnetic device.

41

In January he went to a second weekend intensive, and was again touched by the Guru. Immediately, he felt tingling pain and hot and cold sensations spreading over his upper back and neck. His throat burned and his head and neck moved spontaneously. Next, he felt bliss and inner peace. Later, his head began to spin, and he felt vibrations in his hands. Then his knees burned, and he felt a buzzing up his spine that ended in feelings of light and energy in his head. During all of this his breathing was irregular: at times rapid and shallow, at other times slow and deep. Everything seemed to be breaking loose inside of him, and he felt as though he were in labor. Towards the end of this meditation, he experienced great inner beauty, peace, and a deep knowing of his inmost self, then a total sense of freedom and a feeling of coming home. The next day he had difficulty returning to his usual state. He was uncoordinated, concentrated poorly, and was physically exhausted for several days.

After the January intensive, his meditations continued to deepen. Then, for a few days, his left big toe and left foot hurt. This pain was intense, and penetrated through his foot to his lower leg. Also, he had an ache on the left side of the back of his head which extended through to his eye on this side. The eye would occasionally shut spontaneously. After a few days, this intermittent pain disappeared, and the leg pain, which had resisted all treatment, cleared at about the same time.

In his day to day life, friends and family experienced him as more relaxed. A physical therapist, whom he sees regularly, feels he has become more loose, relaxed, and integrated since all of these experiences. His sense of having come home has grown into a feeling of at oneness with the world. Now, in meditation, itching has developed on his forehead, and occasionally on his cheeks, indicating a further progression in the physio-kundalini circuit.

DISCUSSION

The physio-kundalini complex has a number of characteristic features, both objective and subjective. The typical physio-kundalini progression, as outlined, rarely occurs in practice, but often several of the symptoms do manifest.

If we accept the view that they are the results of the balancing action of kundalini as it removes blocks throughout the system, then individual differences in symptom patterns mean that separate areas are blocked. This may be due to differences in genetic make-up and past history of the persons. Also, these processes may last from a few months to several years. Such differences in time span may be caused by variation in the intensity of meditations and in the total amount of balancing needed.

Often the cycle does not run its normal full course, as already noted. This arrest of the physio-kundalini cycle may occur in those who become fascinated with some particular psychic ability. Such an exclusive focus may interrupt the progression at that particular stage. Further variation occurs over a period of time; the signs and symptoms are not present continuously but come on at intervals, most often in meditation, during quiet time or in sleep.

SUMMARY OF SIGNS AND SYMPTOMS

We have attempted to separate the signs (objective indications) and symptoms (subjective descriptions) into four basic categories: motor, sensory, interpretive, and nonphysiological. These categories are outlined in Table 1, and described in more detail in the following pages.

CATEGORIES OF SIGNS AND SYMPTOMS	DESCRIPTIONS
Motor	Any manifestations which can be independently observed and physically measured.
Sensory	Inner sensations such as lights, sounds, and experiences, normally classed as sensations.
Interpretive	Mental processes which interpret experience.
Non-physiological	Phenomena which, taken at face value as genuine occurrences, must involve factors for which physiological explanations are not sufficient.

Table 1. Descriptions of Signs and Symptoms.

Although we make this four-fold classification for convenience, symptoms in different categories, for example, body movements, tingling, and inner lights, may often be merely different aspects of a single integrated experience. Another difficulty is that some phenomena belong in two or three categories at once: objective heat manifestations under motor and sensory, single seeing under sensory and interpretive, and so on. In these cases we have listed the experiences under each of the applicable headings for ease of reference, but we have discussed them only once.

Motor

Body Movements and Unaccustomed Postures   The movements are spontaneous, although the person may be able to inhibit their occurrence. They may affect any part of the body including the eyes. Movements may be smooth and sinuous, spasmodic and jerky, or vibratory. The body may also assume classic hatha yoga postures and hold them for extended periods. The occurrence, pattern, and intensity of these movements and postures vary greatly from person to person.

Abnormal Breathing Patterns   According to yogic theory, vital energy or *prana,* an aspect of kundalini, enters, leaves, and flows through the body with the breath. Some yogis spend many hours each day for years trying to control the flow of this prana through breathing exercises called *pranayama* (literally, energy control). What we observe clinically in most of our cases, is the spontaneous occurrence of classic pranayama patterns: rapid breathing, shallow breathing, deep breathing, or prolonged retention of breath. Advanced yogis say that this spontaneous occurrence is normal, and that it happens almost regularly in the process of the awakening of the kundalini. They say that deliberate practice of pranayama to accelerate kundalini may be dangerous, and is unnecessary, since it will arise of itself as a part of the kundalini process.

Paralysis   During deep meditation the body sometimes becomes temporarily locked into a certain posture, but this temporary

45

paralysis usually ceases when the meditation is over. The two young women in our case studies who had partial paralysis differ in that their disabilities developed gradually and remained over rather long periods, and also interfered with their normal activities. In both these cases, it abated when we were able to relieve their intense fear of the process through explanations, emotional support, and encouragement. Therefore, it seems likely that their paralysis was a secondary symptom, an hysteria-like reaction, rather than a primary effect of the physio-kundalini process.

Sensory

Body Sensations   The skin or inside of the body may tingle, vibrate, itch or tickle. Apt descriptions are a deep ecstatic tickle and feeling of orgasms. These sensations often start in the feet and legs, or pelvis, and move up the back and neck to the top of the head, down the forehead, over the face, then to the throat, and terminate in the abdomen. The progression is seldom this ordered, but when it is, we consider this a typical physio-kundalini cycle.

Heat and Cold   Extremes of temperature sometimes move through the body but not always in patterns. These changes range from purely subjective sensations to objective manifestations (signs) to apparently supernatural instances of extreme heat. If these instances can be verified, it will be quite a challenge to explain.

Inner Lights and Visions   A variety of lights may appear internally. Muktananda ranges these from the red color the size of the whole body through the white and black spots to the lentil-sized blue pearl. These or other lights are sometimes "seen" to light up specific body areas such as the spine and head. Formed visions may also occur.

Light was prominent in most of the accounts cited from the literature and occurred in most of our own cases. Bucke (1970), a psychiatrist and author of *Cosmic Consciousness,* considers this the most important criterion for calling an experience cosmic. He finds a gradation of these phenomena, from subjective symptoms to objective manifestations, similar to that which we observed for heat. The most subtle were those in which this illumination was just a new way of grasping something, as in the "ah ha!" experience. Others "saw" light internally. In the more remarkable cases those who saw light internally were also able to see a darkened room as illuminated. In the extreme case, witnesses reported seeing a halo of light around the illumined one. It seems likely that the terms "illumined", "enlightened" and other references to light were originally objective descriptions rather than just metaphors.

Sounds   Sounds that are heard internally are not only voices, but include a variety of characteristic noises, such as whistling, hissing, chirping, flute-like and roaring. Sounds were reported by most of our own cases, and varied somewhat with the particular tradition of meditation followed by the individual.

Pains   Pains are often reported in the head, eyes, spine, and other parts of the body. These may begin abruptly, with no apparent cause, and may, after a variable period, cease abruptly and permanently. The experience of the psychologist, who discovered her headaches were caused by her attempts to control the physio-kundalini process, suggests that, in general, pains might be caused by conscious or subconscious resistance to the process, rather than to the action of kundalini itself. They also might occur when the flow of kundalini is especially intense through an area that has not yet been sufficiently opened. This may have been true of the actress.

Interpretive

Unusual or Extreme Emotions   Ecstasy, bliss, peace, love, devotion, joy and cosmic harmony may occur, but also intense fear,

47

anxiety, depression, hatred, and confusion. In general, especially in the early stages of the process any of the normal emotions may be experienced with much greater intensity than usual. Later on, feelings of peace, love, and contentment tend to predominate.

Distortions of Thought Processes Thoughts may speed up, slow down, or stop altogether. They may seem off balance, strange, or irrational. The person may feel close to insanity, may enter complete trance states, or may become impulsive and feel alienated and generally confused. Most of our cases report these thought changes at some phase of the process.

Detachment The individual may feel that he or she is watching all that is happening, including his or her own thoughts and feelings, from a distance, like one detached. The yogis call this condition "witness consciousness". Sometimes, when it is not mentioned directly, its presence may be inferred from phrases such as "the fire of separation" as with the Sufis, or from feelings of great bliss. It differs from aloofness or anxious withdrawal in that it is a dissociation of the separate observer-self from the mental activities that it observes. The activities may continue as usual. Thus, this condition need not interfere with normal functioning.

Dissociation When the withdrawal of the self from active involvement or identification with what it perceives is attained, the state of detachment or witness consciousness occurs. But when it is not in balance, due to deep psychological resistances, to fear and confusion, or to social and other environmental pressures, then negative aspects of the experience may be emphasized. Hysteria or a state akin to schizophrenia may result. Also, the person may become identified with the physio-kundalini process itself in a negative, egotistical way, believing he or she has been divinely chosen for some great mission, perhaps as a savior. Given time and the proper envi-

48

ronmental support, the imbalance is overcome and one finds a more suitable focus for his or her energies, and the negative symptoms vanish.

Single Seeing   This interesting variation in the visual function may be an experience described in the Gospels: "The light of the body is the eye; therefore when thine eye is single thy whole body is also full of light" (Luke 11:34).

Single seeing can be easily identified as a separate and distinct state by the typical and graphic metaphors used to describe the experience by people who have had it. For example, Muktananda said, "My eyes gradually rolled up and became centered . . . Instead of seeing separately . . . they saw as one." Later, in a lecture (February, 1976) he described a state in which his eyes seemed turned equally inward and outward, "seeing"both inner and outer landscapes.

The woman artist said, "My eyes seemed to move separately and the pupils felt like holes which bored into my head and met in the center."

Flora Courtois (1970) wrote,

> My sight had changed, sharpened to an infinitely small point which moved ceaselessly in paths totally free of the old accustomed ones, as if flowing from a new source.
>
> It was as if some inner eye . . . which extended without limit . . . had been restored . . . focused on infinity in a way that was detached from immediate sight and yet had a profound effect on sight . . . there was a sharp one-pointedness to my attention now rooted into some deeper center so that my everyday sight, my eyes, were released from their (need) to see the world outside . . . no matter where I looked no shadow (image) of my nose . . . ever appeared in the clear field of sight.

The above is so close to the psychological process that Jung (1932) speaks of, that his words, spoken at the seminar on kundalini, are used here to amplify and clarify it.   He was asked if it was not Wotan who loses one eye.   He agreed and added that Osiris did also.   He then went on to say:

49

Wotan has to sacrifice his one eye to the well of Mimir, the well of wisdom, which is the unconscious; you see one eye will remain in the depths or turned towards it. Therefore Jakob Boehme, when he was "enchanted into the centre of nature," as he says, wrote his book about the "Reversed Eye;" one of his eyes was turned inward, it kept on looking into the underworld, which amounts to the loss of one eye; he had no longer two eyes for this world.

Jesus uses a parable to tell of his inner truth. Jung uses myth as metaphor for a similar experience of truth at a deep psychological level. In the cases cited here the experience is the truth itself.

In a research setting Alyce Green (1975) reported that some of her biofeedback subjects saw an inner vision of a single eye confronting them while they were deeply relaxed.

Great Body   Experiencing oneself to be larger than the normal size of one's body is occasionally reported.

Non-physiological

Out-of-Body-Experiences   People experiencing this state feel themselves to be in a location away from their physical bodies. At present we must regard these perceptions as subjective, which would make them little different from vivid and involuntary imaginings. However, if it could somehow be verified by independent or objective means, that these people have actually been where they say they have been—if they can alter that place, or retrieve information from it—then this phenomenon would have to be listed also under Sensory and even, perhaps, under Motor. It would also become impossible to explain with current Western models of brain function and mind-body relationship. As in single seeing, the language used to describe this state is so typical that we think of it as quite separable from other states of divided consciousness.

Psychic Perceptions   Psychic abilities and experiences, particularly the obtaining of information through means other than the known physical senses, are frequently reported by people in whom the kundalini awakening process is occurring.   Such experiences, if confirmed, will also have to be listed under Sensory, and, like out-of-the-body experiences, will require explanations going beyond the possibilities of today's neurophysiological models.

Sometimes the perceptions are clearly a result of the kundalini activity.   Often, however, they preceded the awakening, indicating that people are more likely to have the physio-kundalini mechanism triggered if they are naturally psychic. In fact, such people are often so strongly affected by the physio-kundalini forces that their meditations are quite disturbing, and they seek to avoid opening themselves up further to this influence. This attitude usually changes, however, when they learn more about what is happening and become established in a regular, gentle, and reliable meditative practice.

CORRELATION WITH BENTOV'S MODEL

In this section we shall see to what extent Bentov's physiological model for the kundalini process (described in detail in Appendix A) is consistent with, and can account for, our observations. The same names are used to refer to the various signs and symptoms as were used in the previous section.

Motor signs and symptoms   The cerebral current may stimulate the motor cortex or thalamic centers having to do with associated or group muscle movements, such as the posturing reflexes. The apparent non-specificity of some of these movements may indicate that the focus of disturbance is deep in the brain, rather than in the cortex. Breathing patterns may be similarly stimulated, and paralysis is probably a secondary effect as already noted.

Body Sensations   Body sensations may be attributed to direct stimulation of the sensory cortex by the current generated in the cerebral hemispheres. The characteristic sequence of affected body parts corresponds to their sequence of representation in the sensory cortex, as shown in Appendix A, Figure 11: first the toes, then the limbs, back, head, eyes and face, to the throat, and finally the abdominal area represented just above the temporal lobe. According to Bentov's model the earliest body sensations appear in the foot, especially in the left big toe represented in the brain's central sulcus. (The holy river, Ganges, is said to have originated from the large toe of God. In siddha yoga the feet of the Guru are especially venerated, particularly the large toe.) The exact correspondence between the sequence of stimulation in the typical physio-kundalini cycle and the sequence of representation in the sensory cortex gives strong support to at least this aspect of Bentov's model.

It is interesting to note that in this model the throat and abdomen are the last opening sites, thus indicating the completion of the cycle. The importance of the throat is substantiated by the reference to it in the name given to the kundalini in the Hindu scriptures; they call it *Vagshwari*, the Goddess of Speech. Supposedly, it is after the throat opening when all the legendary powers undergo an increase in the adept.

Heat and cold   These may be caused by hypothalamic stimulation. The representation of our body in this area of the brain is less specific than in the cortex, which may explain the lack of regularity in the movement of these sensations. Objective manifestation of extreme heat is difficult to explain with Bentov's model alone. It does not contradict it, but suggests that other factors are also involved in the kundalini phenomenon.

Light and Sound   These could be due to stimulation near the lateral and medial geniculate regions, as well as from standing waves generated in the ventricles. The usual lack of formed elements could be due to the large distance of the circuit from cortical representation for light and sound. Formed visions and voices may indicate spread of stimulation to the more adjacent associative areas for speech, sound, and vision. If they are psychically determined they would have quite a different and unknown origin. Certainly objective manifestations of light, if confirmed, would also require explanations beyond our present knowledge.

Pains   These might occur when the current generated in the brain meets with some resistance that is not easily overcome (a block that is not easily purified out of the system). The perception of the pain may be referred out and seem to come from various parts of the body, or motor stimulation could cause tension, generating pain in the periphery itself. In practice, it makes little difference whether these impurities or blocks to the rise of kundalini are actually in chakras (psychic energy centers) in the spinal canal, as the yogis say, or in peripheral body parts, or in specific brain regions, or at some more subtle level of the mind. These various possibilities are not mutually exclusive, and the net result is the same.

Emotions and Distorted Thought Processes   These are not inconsistent with Bentov's model, but are too complex to be explained by it at this time.

Detachment and Dissociation   Wilder Penfield (1958) reports experiences akin to these upon direct stimulation of area 39 of the cortex. Thus they could be a simple result of the circulating current, or they could have a more subtle psychological origin.

Single Seeing and the Great Body   These are not inconsistent with Bentov's model, but cannot be explained by it at this time.

Out-of Body and Psychic Experiences   Bentov's model does not offer an explanation for these as objectively confirmed phenomena, but it does give guidelines for the direction in which research might profitably move (see Epilogue).

Concluding Comment

Bentov's model is able to account, in detail, for many of the signs and symptoms we have observed. Even if it ultimately proves to be only partially correct, or to explain only a part of the full kundalini phenomenon, it has enormous heuristic value at this state.

What distinguishes Bentov's model from all previous attempts to explain kundalini is that it generates further hypotheses, and suggests a number of experiments to test them. For example:

1.   Measure the very weak magnetic fields around the head of an expert meditator, following such methods as those described by Brenner, Williamson, and Kaufman (1975).

2.   Determine at what stage of meditation the irregular microtremor changes to a resonant vibration.

3.   Develop a biofeedback system to aid meditators in reaching resonance.

4.   Study the effects of magnetic stimulation on one side and then on both sides of the head.

5.   Study light, heat, and sound sensations reported by meditators, and determine which of these can be correlated with physically measurable conditions.

KUNDALINI: CLASSICAL AND CLINICAL

We now have two models of kundalini: the classical yogic description, and Bentov's physiological model, plus our own clinical observations. Those aspects of the process which could have a purely physiological basis, either that which Bentov proposes or some other, we have designated physio-kundalini. The majority of our clinical observations fall within the physio-kundalini category, and we have just examined to what extent they might be accounted for by Bentov's model. But the physio-kundalini process, as we have observed it, differs from the classical yogic description in certain important respects.

Most notable of these is the pathway taken by the kundalini energy or the body sensation as it travels through the system. Classically, the energy awakens at the base of the spine, travels straight up the spinal canal, and has completed its journey when it reaches the top of the head. Along this route, however, there are said to be several chakras, or psychic energy centers, which the kundalini must pass through to reach its goal. These chakras contain impurities that kundalini must remove before it can continue its upward course. On the other hand, in the usual clinical picture, the energy sensation travels up the legs and back to the top of the head, then down the face, through the throat, to a terminal point in the abdomen. What is the relationship between these two descriptions?

We must be aware that yogic descriptions, in addition to being dogmatic, are often very subtle. Western scientists say that the actual location of sensory perception is in the sensory cortex, even though the sensation is felt to be in the periphery. Similarly, the yogis might mean that the sensations, blocks, and openings (such as the throat opening), which are felt to be in various body parts, are in some subtle way represented in the spinal chakras.

Still another possibility is suggested by the experience of one of Muktananda's students (personal communication, 1975) who says he feels energy spreading throughout his body, but especially descending from his forehead over his face to his throat, then to his chest and abdomen, then to the base of his spine, and only then into and up the center of the spine itself. He says the sensation in the spine is more subtle and difficult to perceive than that of the peripheral areas—perhaps because most of the energy has not yet entered his spine.

The time factor is also different in the classical and clinical pictures. All the characteristic elements of the physio-kundalini complex are included in the classic description. And yet, we find quite "ordinary" people who complete the physio-kundalini cycle in a matter of months, whereas yogic scriptures assign a minimum of three years for culmination of full kundalini awakening in the case of the most advanced initiates. Here we have the suggestion that full kundalini awakening included a larger complex of which the physio-kundalini process is only a part.

It is too early to say exactly what the relationships are, except that perhaps the physio-kundalini mechanism is a separate entity which may be activated as part of a full kundalini awakening. Much of the problem stems from the difficulty of comparing different stages when many processes are happening concurrently. Individual differences complicate the picture. But it would be possible to clarify things by remembering the theoretical definition of kundalini action as a purificatory process. If the impurities or imbalances have any objective reality, it should be possible to demonstrate them with physiological and psychological tests, and to correlate their removal with specific signs and symptoms observed clinically. Since we now know that the process may be triggered (see Appendix A), and how it may be recognized in its initial stages, long-term case studies, covering the entire course of the process, are a logical next step in these investigations. They would be invaluable in documenting specific objective ways in which the kundalini process is beneficial.

DIAGNOSTIC CONSIDERATIONS

Our results indicate a clear distinction between the physio-kundalini complex and psychosis, and provide a number of criteria for distinguishing between these two states. We have seen, in some of our cases, that a schizophrenic-like condition can result when the person undergoing the kundalini experience receives negative feedback either from social pressure or from the resistances of his or her own earlier conditioning.

Evidence that these states are distinct and separate comes from two of our cases, the woman artist and another we did not discuss, who became "psychotic" after being confined to a mental institution for inappropriate behavior. Each of them reported that during their stay in their respective mental institutions they were quite sure that they (and several of the other patients) could tell which of their number were "crazy" and which of them were just "far-out and turned on". Possibly this is a situation where "it takes one to know one", and a person whose own kundalini has been awakened can intuitively sense the kundalini state of another. This is of special interest, as it may point to a use of such people in assisting to decide which way the balance lies between the two processes in any particular patient (see Appendix B).

Clinicians usually have a finely tuned sense of what is psychotic. Mainly, it is this sense for the smell of psychosis that tells us if the patients are unbalanced in this way, or are instead inundated with more positive psychic forces. Also, there is a feeling for whether they are dangerous to themselves and others. Persons in the early phases of kundalini awakening, if hostile or angry, are, in our experience, rarely inclined to act out.

Also, those in whom the kundalini elements predominate are usually much more objective about themselves, and have an interest in sharing what is going on in them. Those on the psychotic side tend to be very oblique, secretive and totally preoccupied with ruminations about some vague but significant subjective aspect of their experience which they can never quite communicate to others.

With our own results and Bentov's model, we have several more distinguishing features. Sensations of heat are common in these high states, but are rare in psychosis. Also very typical are feelings of vibrations or flutterings, tinglings and itchings that move in definite patterns over the body, usually in the sequence described

57

earlier. But these patterns may be irregular in atypical cases or in those who have preconceived ideas of how the energies should circulate. With all this, bright lights may be seen internally. There may be pains, especially in the head, which suddenly arise or cease during critical phases in the process. Unusual breathing patterns are common, as well as other spontaneous movements of the body. Noises such as chirping and whistling sounds are heard, but seldom do voices intrude in a negative way as in psychosis. When voices are heard, they are perceived to come from within and are not mistaken for outer realities.

RECOMMENDATIONS AND FURTHER DISCUSSION

Our results support the view that this force is positive and creative. Each one of our own cases is now successful on his or her own terms. They all report that they handle stress more easily, and are more fulfilled than ever before in relationships with others. The classical cases indicate that special powers, as well as deep inner peace, may result from culmination of the full kundalini process. But in the initial stages, stress of the experience itself, coupled with a negative attitude from oneself or others, may be overwhelming and cause severe imbalance.

Experience suggests an approach of understanding, strength, and gentle support. The spontaneous trances, which disturbed our case of the writer, ceased when we encouraged him to enter a trance state voluntarily. By recognizing a distinction between psychotic and psychically active, we had communicated to him an attitude that the trances were valid and meaningful. Because of our own acceptance of the condition, the patient also was able to accept it. The trances themselves ceased to control him as soon as he gave up his own resistance to them and the forces behind them. Similarly, the psychologist had severe headaches, but these stopped as soon as she ceased trying to control the process and simply went with it.

The pain, in other words, resulted not from the process itself but from her resistance to it. We suspect this is true of all the negative effects of the physio-kundalini process.

Symptoms, when caused by this process, will disappear spontaneously in time. Because it is essentially a purificatory or balancing process, and each person has only a finite amount of impurities of the sort removed by kundalini, the process is self-limiting. Disturbances seen are therefore not pathological, but rather therapeutic, constituting a removal of potentially pathological elements. The kundalini force arises spontaneously from deep within the mind, and is apparently self-directing. Tension and imbalance thus result, not from the process itself, but from conscious or subconscious interference with it. Helping the person to understand and accept what is happening to him or to her may be the best that we can do.

Usually the process, left to itself, will find its own natural pace and balance. But if it has already become too rapid and violent, our experience suggests it may be advisable to take steps such as heavier diet, suspension of meditations, and vigorous physical activity, to moderate its course.

The people, in whom the physio-kundalini process is most easily activated, and in whom it is most likely to be violent and disturbing, are those with especially sensitive nervous systems—the natural psychics. Many of our cases had some psychic experience prior to their awakening. Natural psychics often find the physio-kundalini experience so intense that they will not engage in the regular classical meditation methods that usually further the kundalini process; instead, they either refrain from meditation or adopt some mild form of their own devising. But much of their anxiety may be due to misunderstanding and ignorance of the physio-kundalini process. Rather than increasing their fear, we should be giving them the knowledge and confidence to allow the process to progress at the maximum comfortable, natural rate.

Much could be accomplished by changing attitudes, first around people experiencing the kundalini, but ultimately in society as a whole. This is not just for the person's benefit, but for all of us who need models in our own spiritual search. Some other cultures are more advanced than our own in terms of their recognition of the positive value of spiritually or psychically developed people.

The trance state in Bali serves an important adaptive function for the children. In parts of Africa, trance is a social and religious necessity, required for kundalini arousal (Katz 1973).

In South Africa, a state, which Western psychiatry would probably call an acute schizophrenic break, is a prerequisite for initiation into the priesthood by one Kalahari tribe (Skutch 1974).

Here we must speak of the many creative people who are now suffering because of mistakes that we in the healing professions have made in the past. We have a special obligation to make every effort to correct those mistakes. At this time in our society it could be that such charismatic and strangely acting people as Shamans, trance mediums, and *Masts* (the God-intoxicated) might find themselves in custodial care. Possibly there are many now so situated who could be found and released to more positive uses among us. The problem is to recognize them among the other inmates of our institutions. Here Meher Baba's work with *Masts* (Donkin, 1948) would be a useful precedent to study (see Appendix B). If it is true that, to a certain extent, it takes one to know one, a special and invaluable use for people who have already experienced the physio-kundalini process would be to assist us in such a project.

There are many undergoing this process who at times feel quite insane. When they behave well and keep silent they may avoid being called schizophrenic, or being hospitalized, or sedated. Nevertheless their isolation and sense of separation from others may cause them much suffering. We must reach such people, their families, and society, with information to help them recognize their condition as a blessing, not a curse.

60

Certainly we must no longer subject people, who might be in the midst of this rebirth process, to drugs or shock therapies, approaches which are at opposite poles to creative self-development.

These people though confused, fearful, and disoriented, are already undergoing a therapy from within, far superior to any that we yet know how to administer from without.

KUNDALINI AS THERAPY

I am now in contact with several people of special interest as examples of the kundalini as therapy from within.

A 54 year old male psychologist-writer was hospitalized for three months twenty years ago with a psychotic break, characterized by disturbances in judgement, flight of ideas, grandiosity, and over-activity. After this episode he suffered from a chronic mild depression and had been somewhat unstable. Nevertheless, he made his living as a therapist, occasionally being very effective, but constantly becoming involved in counter transference problems (over-involvement with his clients). At other times he was unable to provide for himself adequately.

About two years ago, he became a disciple of Muktananda, a yogi master. He found his stay at the ashram, and the contact with other devotees and the Guru, to be a very powerful therapy. Signs of kundalini awakening began early in his stay there, and led to, or at least was accompanied by, a prodigious increase in productivity in his writing, new depths of interpersonal satisfactions, and a more sure grasp on his life. I saw him frequently, before and during this important period, and can attest to the dramatic strengthening of his whole personality structure, character, and ways of dealing with his inner and outer worlds.

A 44 year old woman psychologist had been severely depressed for many years and in the last eleven years she made two serious suicide attempts by overdosing on sleeping pills. She remained in coma for several days following each of these episodes. Her only extended hospitalization for her depression followed the birth of her first child in 1956, prior to the suicide attempts. For years she held a responsible position as an administrator and was a successful psychotherapist. During this time she herself was undergoing psychotherapy, including a classical psychoanalysis.

There is a history of suicide in her family, including the suicide death of her grandfather. In 1972, her oldest daughter, who was sixteen, killed herself. Within a few months, this woman attended a meditation retreat where she spent many hours each day in meditation. Within a short time, she began to have spontaneous kundalini experiences. She is now also a disciple of Swami Muktananda and is planning an extended stay at his ashram in India.

I have known her since 1973. During the first year of our acquaintance she was somewhat withdrawn and reserved. In the past two years, she has truly blossomed into a secure, intact, fun loving person. She tells me that she has not known a day of depression in the past two years. My observations confirm this self-appraisal.

I recall four other psychics, each of whom had some sort of convulsive disorder diagnosed and treated by competent physicians. In each of these persons there was marked relief in symptoms and their need for anti-convulsive drugs, after finding and using their psychic talents. Some other creative pursuit might have been equally freeing. These four chose to become professional psychics, and although no claim is made on this evidence for a causal relationship between their new energy investment and the amelioration of their symptoms, it is suggestive. I feel quite certain that at the higher level of functioning that may open up to persons who embark on the kundalini path, there eventually will be many fruits such as better health and emotional balance.

On the other hand, the kundalini process is disruptive and the person undergoing it feels its far-reaching physical and psychological effects. If the person is alone, he or she will suffer doubts and fears that could easily be handled in a supportive Ashram atmosphere, where these disturbing events are accepted and even welcomed.

Without such a setting, those who experience this force may react in a number of ways. Naive persons may interpret the experience as an inner change so profound and upsetting as to be a convincing indication of loss of sanity. This is essentially what happened in our first and third cases, the woman artist and the actress. Also our twelfth case, the middle-aged housewife, suffered these doubts, but dealt with her turmoil by becoming inflated and grandiose.

The woman psychologist handled her inner disruption by becoming part of various groups, with more or less understanding of what she was enduring, and by finding supportive teachers or therapists. It was necessary for her to provide these aids for a year or more before continuing on her own. The scientist, whose understanding was even more adequate and whose situation was quite nourishing, was able to function by simply cutting down on the intensity of his meditations.

It should now be clear that physicians are well advised to be alert for symptom patterns suggestive of kundalini arising. The physician should inquire about his or her meditation practice, but realize that it is not a necessary prerequisite to kundalini awakening. In addition to psychotherapy, if indicated, we recommend that persons suspected of kundalini problems be urged to see someone with kundalini experience, as well.

The selection of this helping person may be most difficult. Unless the physician is experienced and has explored the available resources, the physician may be unable to do more than recommend that the patient seek such a person. The final choice can be best made by the person.

Zen or Transcendental Meditation supervised by a competent teacher, or spontaneous awakening by the direct influence of an enlightened Guru, such as Muktananda, are methods with which we are acquainted. There may be other resources that are equal or superior to these, but which we have not experienced.

We especially want to caution that, methods designed specifically to hasten kundalini arousal, such as the yogic breath-control exercises known as pranayama, should be considered hazardous, unless practiced directly under the guidance of a teacher, or Guru, who is fully realized. Advanced yogis say that these techniques are practiced mainly by those people, who may have heard about the special yogic breathing patterns, without realizing that these patterns occur spontaneously, through natural kundalini arousal as seen in our own cases. Deliberate practice of these methods, by forcing the kundalini, may cause premature and imbalanced release of titanic inner forces. On the other hand, these profound changes can readily be enlisted in a self-healing process as seen in these last three cases.

Neurologists with diagnostic problems that mimic pathologic conditions may gain valuable diagnostic clues by reviewing the patients meditation history, and so avoid altogether, or delay, harsh diagnostic procedures.

Psychotherapists dealing with hysterical overlays, or psychotic reactions to kundalini awakening, are reminded that underneath the neurosis, or psychosis, a process is occurring that is far beyond our ordinary understanding of psychopathology and ecstatic religious states, that William James (1929) and others describe.

SUMMARY

A new clinical entity, the rebirth process. is defined and documented. It is a dynamic, self-directed, self-limited process of mental and physiological purfication, leading to a healthier and more developed state than what we usually consider normal. It has many characteristic features which may be objectively demonstrated. A cross-cultural survey reveals that this process is essentially similar in a wide variety of spiritual traditions. Although it was rare in the West as recently as a few decades ago, it now appears with increasing frequency.

Individuals who experience this transformation and do not understand what is happening sometimes feel they are going insane. This is because the early stages are often marked by great stress, confusion, disorientation, and schizophrenic-like symptoms. Tragically in these cases, clinicians have occasonally mistaken the rebirth process for acute schizophrenia. Some of these patients have been sent to situations destructive to their development, resulting in a great loss, not only to themselves, but also to the society which could have benefited so much from their great creative potential.

A physio-kundalini model for the rebirth process recently proposed by Itzhak Bentov (Appendix A) is evaluated in the light of our results. His model is based on evidence that meditation leads to progressive entrainment of five series-linked harmonic oscillators within the body, beginning with the heart-aortal rhythm and ending with circular electric currents, and their attendant magnetic fields generated within the brain. He postulates that the so-called kundalini effects are the result of direct action of these various oscillators upon the brain. His work is important in that it proposes the first physiological kundalini model based on laboratory measurements and subject to experimental verification.

A second appendix describes the Masts or God-intoxicated ones of India, suggesting that kundalini arousal could soon create similar great beings in the West. A third appendix discusses the nature of intuitive sensitivity in the human organism. We show that the painful and difficult rebirth process is necessary only because the natural growth of this innate ability is unnaturally curtailed by the emotional stresses of mechanistic culture imposed upon our children, causing them to lose this most precious genetic birthright.

Two further appendices are intended as guides for researchers and therapists.

In this book, on the basis of our own clinical experience, we offer many criteria for recognizing the rebirth process and distinguishing it from psychosis, even when these two conditions have temporarily merged.

The complex, which we designate the physio-kundalini complex, typically begins with an energy-sensation which ascends from the legs to the trunk and back, and over the head, then descends to the throat, and then to the termination in the abdomen. Accompanying this progression, which may last from weeks to several years, are a diversity of signs and symptoms. These vary with the individual, but often include heat, pains, spontaneous body movements, unusual breathing patterns, and sensing of inner lights and sounds. These symptoms are not continuously present, but usually occur during meditations or times of rest, and cease when the process is completed.

The course of this development is encouraged by regular meditations under competent guidance, but it may be severely distorted if forced by more powerful methods. Fear and resistance to the process also are major causes of negative reactions. In cases where the process has already become disruptive, a return to balance can usually be brought about by rational explanations, a positive attitude, and emotional support.

The complex closely resembles the state of kundalini awakening described in schools of yoga. Because the yogic kundalini state deals with specific body parts and processes, it lends itself naturally to physiological interpretation and is well suited to account for the objective patterns observed clinically. However, differences from the traditional kundalini concept lead us to propose the term physio-kundalini to describe our own findings.

EPILOGUE

In the laboratories of science it is something of a truism that many experiments with subtle, surprising, and unexplained outcomes remain unpublished while the balance, which support particular hypotheses, get printed. Not mentioned in the body of this book are the results we got in H. Motoyama's laboratory in Japan that showed amplitude differences in the body's micro-motions on the right and left sides of the head. The motion on the left was fifty percent greater. Shortly after we noted this finding, another remarkable event occurred; as the subject went deep into meditation these right-left differences became nearly equal.

In ordinary consciousness the EEG amplitude at one side of the brain is greater than that at the other. With feedback and patience a person can balance these differences, and at that point he or she feels profound peace and tranquility. Perhaps our finding is a physical counterpart of this psychological event.

J. Millay (1976) stated that subjective reports of peacefulness, centeredness, and light were common among a group of students who achieved 7- to 13-Hz EEG phase coherence between right and left brain hemispheres, using biofeedback techniques.

Another confirmation of the link between mental states and body physiology is seen in the work of Manfred Clynes (Jonas, 1972). He has shown that an emotion can be recorded by a simple transducer sensitive to lateral and vertical pressure. Clynes has his subject fantasize the emotion and press on the transducer simultaneously. This creates a characteristic signature or waveform for each emotion.

Brody and Axelrad noted in 1971 that fetal responses they studied had pattern, direction, and effect. Later, Condon and Sanders found that the apparent random movements of infants coordinated with speech sounds they heard. Pearce (1975), in summarizing their work, said, ". . . as adults, each of us has just such a repertoire of micromuscular movements coordinating with our use of and reception to speech." These studies are further evidence for a sensory-motor link similar to those we mentioned here.

We and others have attempted to measure physiological correlates of meditators' reported sensations of heat, light, and sound. As noted in the case histories of meditators undergoing the kundalini awakening process, we did observe temperature changes in one case. Such changes could be made visible on recently developed medical thermographic equipment, without the need for attaching temperature transducers to meditators' bodies. Other experimenters, particularly R. Dobrin (1975) have described the use of sensitive photo-multiplier tubes to detect low-intensity ultraviolet light from the bodies of experimental subjects, but little attention has so far been given to correlating such measurements with meditative processes. Our attempts to measure physiological correlates of meditators' sound sensations were unsuccessful.   Further work along all of these lines, using improved equipment and experimental procedures, may be of great interest in showing the extent to which there is an objective basis for the subjective reports of meditators.

We did an interesting experiment—which has not, to our know-ledge, been confirmed or replicated—using H. Motoyama's electric field sensor, or "chakra measuring device".   When the subject sat quietly in this machine, we could observe the usual EEG waveform. After a few minutes of deep meditation, probably at the point where he feels he has transcended, there suddenly appeared a diminution of these signals, and a corresponding increase in amplitude in a higher frequency band, one which our experimenters had not been equipped to detect.   To our surprise, this new waveform was in the frequency range of 350 to 500 Hz, much higher than the 0-to-50 Hz frequency range of a normal EEG waveform. These higher frequency EEG signals could be an easily measured physi-ological indicator of certain meditative states and out-of-the-body ex-periences, or bilocation of consciousness. If so, a subject full of mystery and fascination for centuries now becomes a new frontier for researchers.

A laboratory in Massachusetts, and two in California (Santa Rosa and San Francisco), with which the author is associated, are testing meditators, using methods described in this book, and others more recently developed, to give immediate audible feedback to show a meditator when his or her body reaches a state of resonant oscillation.

Further steps in our research program may include low-level magneto-encephalograph tests of both meditators and non-meditators, in a special shielded enclosure, and other physical measurements and collection of clinical observations, to extend our understanding of the physio-kundalini process.

APPENDIX A

MICROMOTION OF THE BODY AS A FACTOR IN THE DEVELOPMENT OF THE NERVOUS SYSTEM

Itzhak Bentov
241 Glezen Lane, Wayland, MA 01778

Introduction

In the last few years, both young and old people in the United States and in Europe have taken up the practice of meditation. Regular practice of meditation has a calming and stabilizing effect on its practitioners (4, 13, 14). With prolonged practice, many physiological changes occur in the body. Among them is a change in the mode of functioning of the nervous system. These changes can be monitored by the application of a modified ballistocardiograph to a seated upright subject.

Theoretically, when meditation is practiced properly, a sequence of strong and unusual bodily reactions and unusual psychological states is eventually triggered.* Most meditators realize that these reactions are caused by meditation and don't become alarmed. However, sometimes this mechanism can be triggered in nonmeditators. Our observations indicate that exposure to certain

---

* The "rising of kundalini", as described in classical yoga literature, is a stimulus or "energy" activating a "center" (chakra) at the base of the spine and working its way up the spine. The stimulus stops at several centers along the spine, as it rises. These centers are located opposite the major nerve plexuses in the abdomen and in the thorax, which are also stimulated in the process. Eventually the stimulus ends up in the head. Along its path, it often causes violent motion in some parts of the body, signifying that there is "resistance" to its passage. The rising of the kundalini may happen suddenly or over a period of several years. After entering the head, the stimulus continues down the face into the larynx, and the abdominal cavity.

mechanical vibrations, electromagnetic waves, or sounds may trigger this mechanism. It is the purpose of this article to bring to the attention of the medical profession this mechanism and some of its symptoms.

Summary

The ballistocardiogram of a sitting subject, who is capable of altering his or her state of consciousness at will, shows a rhythmic sine wave pattern when the subject is in a deep meditative state. This is attributed to the development of a standing wave in the aorta, which is reflected in the rhythmic motion of the body. This reasonating oscillator (the heart-aorta system) will rhythm entrain four additional oscillators, eventually resulting in a fluctuating magnetic field around the head.

Our initial experiments indicate that the five resonating systems are:

1. Heart-aorta system producing an oscillation of about 7 Hz in the skeleton, including the skull. The upper part of the body also has a resonant frequency of about 7 Hz.

2. The skull accelerates the brain up and down, producing acoustical plane waves reverberating through the brain at KHz frequencies.

3. These acoustical plane waves are focused by the skull onto the ventricles, thus activating and driving standing waves within the third and lateral ventricles.

4. Standing waves within the cerebral ventricles in the audio and supersonic ranges stimulate the sensory cortex mechanically, resulting eventually in a stimulus traveling in a closed loop around each hemisphere. Such a traveling stimulus may be viewed as a "current".

5. As a result of these circular "currents", each hemisphere produces a pulsating magnetic field. These fields are of opposing polarities.

This magnetic field—radiated by the head acting as an antenna—interacts with the electric and magnetic fields already in the environment. We may consider the head as simultaneously a transmitting and receiving antenna, tuned to a particular one of the several resonant frequencies of the brain. Environmental fields may thus be fed back to the brain, thus modulating that resonant frequency. The brain will interpret this modulation as useful information.

This paper presents a preliminary report on the possible mechanism of the so-called "kundalini". The kundalini effect is viewed by the author as part of the development of the nervous system. This development can be elicited by the practice of any of several different types of meditative techniques, or it may develop spontaneously. Research into this area is continuing and investigation of the kundalini effect by different methods is in progress.

Micromotion Measurement with the Capacitive Probe

Small body motions accompanying the motion of blood through the circulatory system may be measured with a capacitive probe apparatus. A subject sits on a chair between two metal plates, one above the head, and one under the seat, 5 to 10 cm from the body.

The two plates of the capacitor are part of a tuned circuit. The movement of the subject will modulate the field between the two plates. This signal is processed and fed into a single channel recorder, which registers both the motion of the chest due to respiration and the movement of the body reacting to the motion of the blood in the heart-aorta system. The resulting recording trace (Figure 2) is very similar to that of a ballistocardiogram (3), in which the subject lies on a platform, to which are attached 3 mutually perpendicular accelerometers or strain gauges, to measure the body's motion in response to blood flow. But in the capacitive probe measurements, gravitational forces and the elasticity of the skeleton and the general body build play important roles.

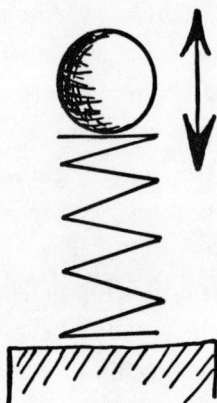

Figure 1. Mass on a spring.

As an analogy, a seated subject can be represented by a mass on a spring (Figure 1): the spring is the spinal column and the mass is the weight of the upper part of the body. Upon the ejection of blood from the heart, this mass is set into motion and starts oscillating at its natural frequency when the person is in a deep meditative state.

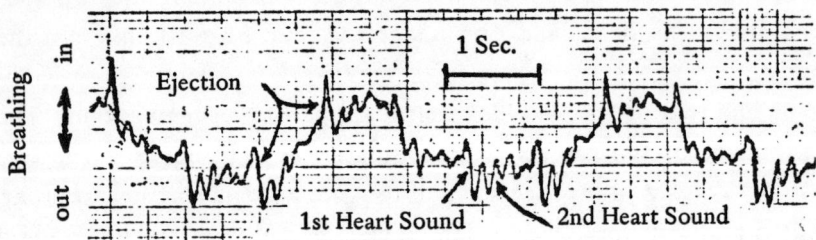

Figure 2. Baseline resting state record.

Figure 2 shows a baseline resting state record, in which the micromotion of the body is superimposed over the motion of the chest, caused by breathing. These are the large slow waves of about a

3 second period, or 20 breaths/minute. The first 7 Hz wave is caused by the ejection of blood from the left ventricle, which makes the body recoil downward and sets the body oscillating. The second wave corresponds closely to the action of the blood flowing through the aortic arch, lifting the body up. The third wave occurs at about the same time as the closing of the aortic valve and the slight back-flow of the blood, called the dichrotic notch. The first and third waves correspond closely to the first and second heart sounds.

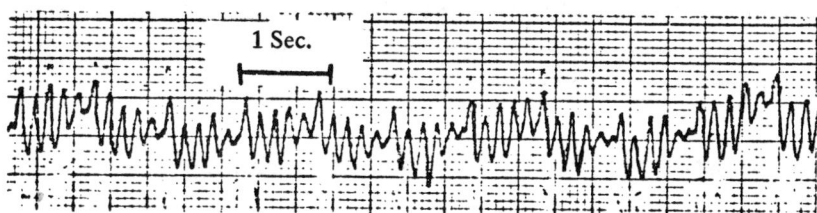

Figure 3. Deep meditative state record.

Figure 3 shows a recording, in which the subject is in a deep meditative state, a few minutes after the baseline reading. Breathing is very shallow, as shown by the practically even level of the 7.5-Hz waves. The irregularity, which characterized the baseline behavior (Figure 2) is gone. Large amplitude regular waves—practically pure sine waves—are present. An almost pure sine wave is what characterizes this state. The body moves in a simple harmonic motion.

Figure 4 shows the return to baseline of the same subject.

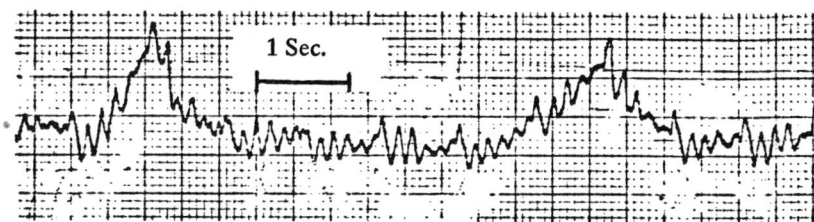

Figure 4. Return to baseline resting state record.

Breathing is deeper again, the irregularity of the wave pattern is back, but is not as irregular as before. Total elapsed time for the recording was about twenty minutes.

We have noticed that the regularity in rhythm is obtained at the expense of breathing. The subject can stay in the shallow breathing state for a long time without having to compensate later by deep rapid breathing. This is a state in which the demand for oxygen by the body seems to be lowered. If one stops breathing for a while without being in a deep meditative state (4), the same regular pattern will be achieved. However, oxygen deficiency builds up quickly and overbreathing will be necessary to restore balance, while in the meditative state this overbreathing does not occur.

The Development of a Standing Wave in the Aorta

The regular movement of the body indicates that a standing wave is set up in the vascular system, specifically, in the aorta (5, 6). This is the only feasible explanation of the regular sine wave-like behavior of the body. This standing wave, as will be shown later, has far-reaching consequences and affects several other resonant systems in the body, which are all driven by this large signal.

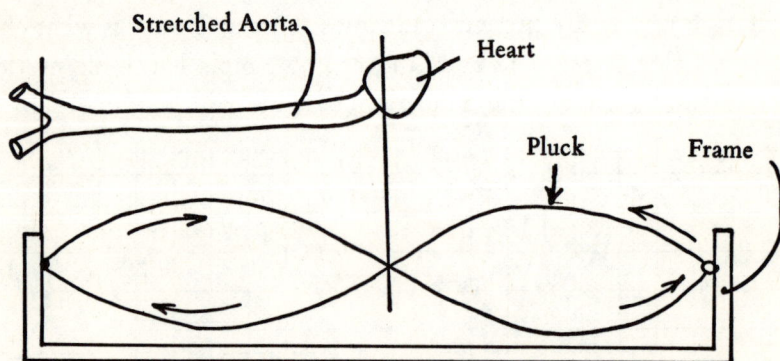

Figure 5a. Comparison of the aorta to a stretched vibrating string. The length of the stretched aorta is equal to one half the wave length of the string.

The aorta is the major artery of the body. When the left ventricle of the heart ejects blood, the aorta, being elastic, balloons out just distal to the ventricle. Under these conditions, a pressure pulse travels down along the aorta. When the pressure pulse reaches the iliac bifurcation, part of it rebounds and starts traveling up the aorta (Figure 5a, 5b). When the timing of the pressure pulses traveling down the aorta coincides or is in phase with the reflected pressure pulses, a standing wave is achieved. This standing wave of approximately 7 Hz will cause the body to move in a rhythmic fashion, provided the aorta is properly tuned. Presumably, a feedback loop is set up between the bifurcation and the heart, which then regulates the breathing so as to make the lungs and the diaphragm contact the aorta and regulate its impedance. This allows the pressure pulse to be in phase with both the ejection and the dichrotic notch. This is an entirely automatic process during deep meditation.

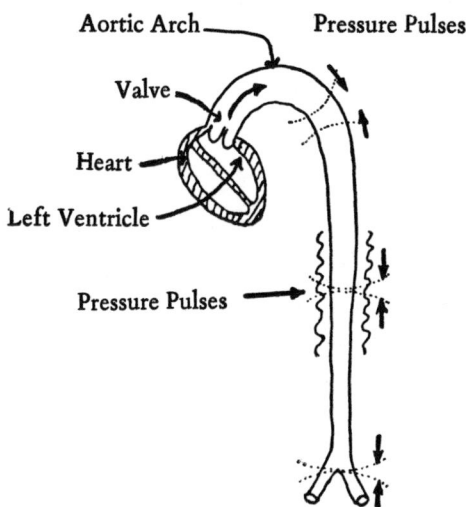

Figure 5b. Collision of the oppositely travelling pressure pulses causes a destructive interference pattern and vibration of aortic walls.

Acoustical Plane Waves in the Body

The movement of the body is relatively small, 0.003 to 0.009 mm, but the body and particularly the head are very dense, tight structures. By moving up and down, the skull accelerates the brain with a mild impact in both directions (Figure 6). This sets up acoustical and possible electrical plane waves reverberating within the skull. The brain may be considered as a piezoelectric gel, converting mechanical vibrations into electrical vibrations, and conversely.

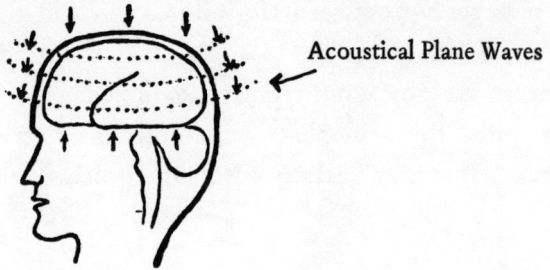

Figure 6. Acoustical plane waves moving through the brain.

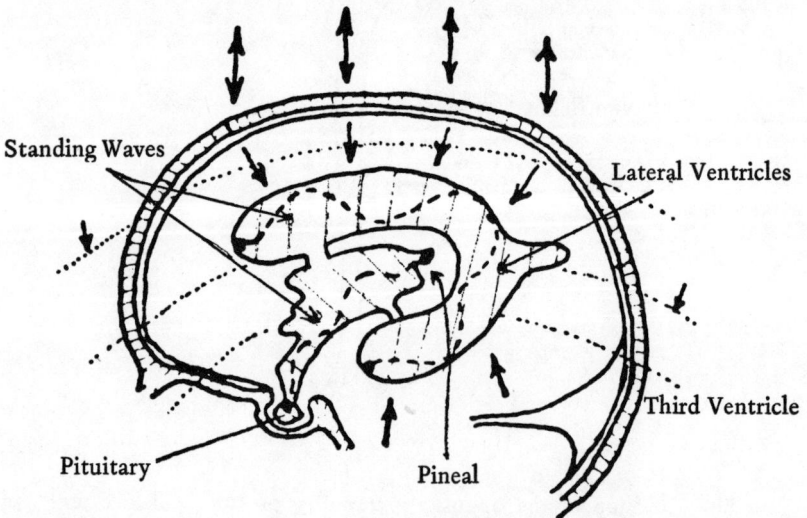

Figure 7. Lateral cross section of brain, showing acoustical standing waves.

The acoustical plane waves reflected from the cranial vault are focused upon the third and the lateral ventricles, as shown in Figures 7 and 8 (7). High-frequency acoustical waves generated by the heart are reflected from the cranial vault and are focused upon the third and lateral ventricles of the brain.

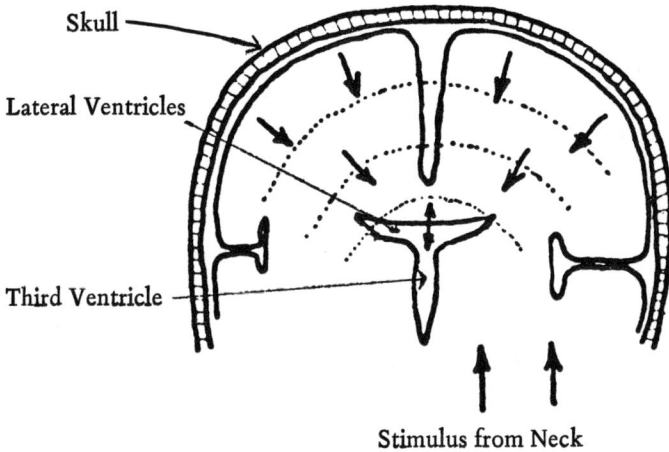

Figure 8. Frontal cross section of brain.

Acoustical Standing Waves in the Ventricles

A hierarchy of frequencies couples the 7 Hz body movement to the higher frequencies in the ventricles.

The body can be considered as a bag of elastic skin containing stiff gel and supported by a rigid armature. The motion of the heart-aorta system sets this gel vibrating in different modes. Assuming the velocity of signal propagation to be 1200m/sec. the fundamental frequencies for the different parts of the body would be along the vertical axis of the body: (1) brain, 4000 Hz; (2) circumference of skull, 2250 Hz; (3) whole body length, 375 Hz; (4) trunk and head, 750 Hz; (5) heart sounds, 35 to 2000 Hz (20)*.

Part of the energy of the acoustical waves coming from the cranial vault is reflected from the interface of the ventricles and sets the cerebrospinal fluid vibrating. The calculated fundamental frequency of the lateral ventricles is 4000 Hz and that of the third ventricle, 12000 Hz. These are the basic standing waves within the ventricles. Again, as long as the body is in a deep meditative state, it is assumed that these two oscillators stay locked in step with the heart sounds. This phase-locking may occur with the high-frequency end of the heart sounds, i.e. above the 2000-Hz range. The vibrations produced in the brain tissue by the standing waves in the ventricles are conducted to the middle ear and converted into sound. This is the sound that will be recognized by the meditator as an "inner sound" (Figure 9). These sounds may start abruptly, last for a few seconds or minutes, and die out.

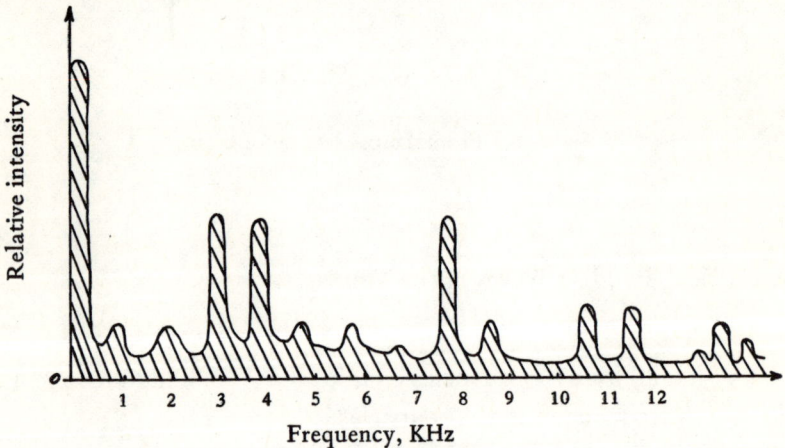

Figure 9. Frequency distribution of "inner sounds" heard by meditators.

* The high-frequency component of the heart sounds, although very low in intensity, may be able to drive the ventricles directly. The stimulus will be conducted by the left side of the neck, up into the skull, and reflected back from the cranial vault to the ventricles.

Frequency distribution measurements of "inner sounds" reported by 156 meditators are made by asking each meditator to compare the sounds heard during meditation with sounds produced by an audio-frequency oscillator through an earphone in one ear. The subject rotates the oscillator frequency control to match oscillator tones with those heard or remembered as the "inner sound". The frequency distribution is not smooth, but shows several sharp peaks, harmonics of the fundamental frequency, and possibly beat frequencies produced between the third and lateral ventricles of the brain, which are connected by a fluid bridge. In the frequency range below 1 KHz, acoustical standing waves running through the entire body, and the higher harmonics of the heart beat and the heart sounds appear.

The Circular Sensory Cortex "Current"

Figure 10 shows a lateral or side view of the brain. A cross section of the left hemisphere, along line AB through the sensory cortex, is shown as Figure 11 (7). The labels in Figure 11 show sensory cortex areas corresponding to specific sensory functions, and to three pleasure centers, which elicit pleasurable sensations when stimulated. These are: (1) cingulate gyrus; (2) lateral hypothalamus; (3) hippocampus and amygdala areas.

Just above the roof of the lateral ventricle starts the medial fissure, the cleft which separates the two hemispheres.

When a standing wave is present in the ventricles, the roof of the lateral ventricles acts as a taut skin on a drum that moves rapidly up and down, as shown in the sketch (Figure 8).

The roof of the lateral ventricles is the corpus callosum, a bundle of nerve fibers connecting the two hemispheres (7). The vibration of the corpus callosum and of the brain mass in general may serve as a pace-setter in the phase synchronization which occurs between the two hemispheres during meditation (13).

81

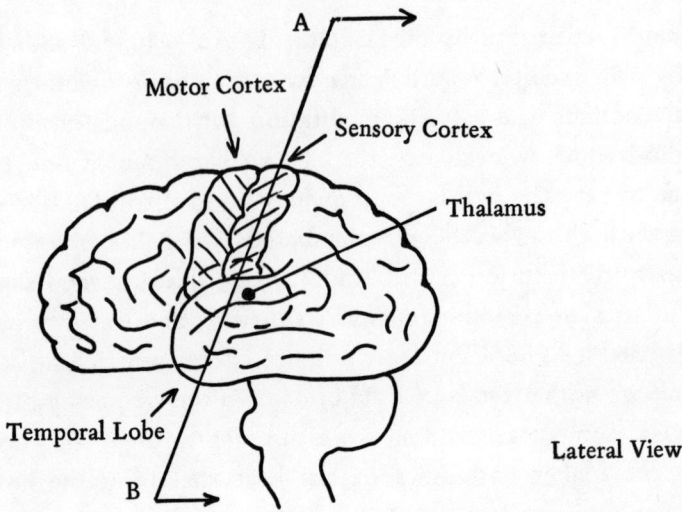

Figure 10. Lateral view of the brain, with section line AB.

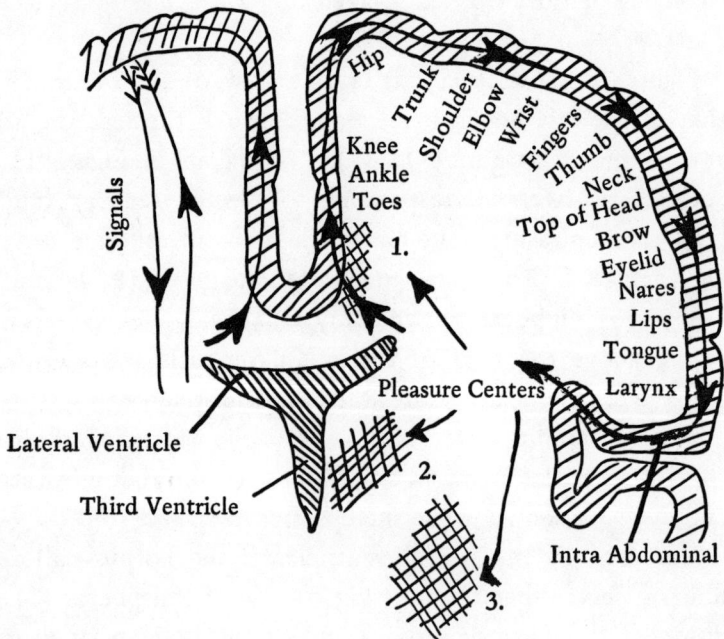

Figure 11.   Cross section of the left hemisphere of the brain, through section line AB of Figure 10.

When the sensory cortex is stimulated electrically or mechanically, paresthesias occur in the area of the body corresponding to certain points on the cortex. These points are mapped out on the surface of the cortex as shown in Figure 11. As the roof of the lateral ventricles vibrates, it stimulates first the toes, then the ankles, then the calves, thighs, and as the stimulus rounds the corner of the hemisphere, the pelvis is stimulated. As the stimulus spreads along the cortex, it will affect the trunk, moving along the spine towards the head.

The cortex has different acoustical properties from the white matter and the cerebrospinal fluid. The white matter is made up mostly of myelinated fibers, a fatty substance which will tend to damp out an acoustical signal. The cortex may be viewed as a water-based gel that conducts vibration well.

Thus, an acoustical interface exists between the white matter, the cortex, and the cerebrospinal fluid. The cortex will therefore preferentially tunnel the acoustical signal.

This mechanical vibratory action is assumed to cause electrical polarization of the tissue of the cortex, to allow enhanced conductivity of the tissue to the stimulus moving along the cortex. This moving stimulus may be viewed as a current. According to our hypothesis, this current is responsible for the effects of the "awak-" ened kundalini" on the body (11, 12).

Sensory signals usually come to the cortex through the thalamus and go back the same way (Figures 10, 11). It is interesting to note that those parts of the body, which are represented on the surface of the cortex facing the cranium, are felt more strongly by a person experiencing the kundalini stimulus. Those chakras,* or energy centers, are most actively felt, while portions of the cortex,

---

* Chakras are, according to the classical descriptions in oriental literature, energy centers, which connect the individual to cosmic energy sources. There are seven of them and they are associated with major nerve centers and the endocrine glands.

which are cushioned and are located inside the folds of the brain, are less noticeable to the individual. This may well occur because the arch between the tops of the two hemispheres and the temporal areas are exposed to a double stimulus—one coming up from the ventricles and one coming down from the cranial vault, accelerating the brain downward. The larynx is the last point on the cortex facing the skull, and it is also the last chakra to be activated and strongly felt. Presumably, the stimulus continues inside the fold of the temporal lobe and closes the circuit, as shown in Figure 12.

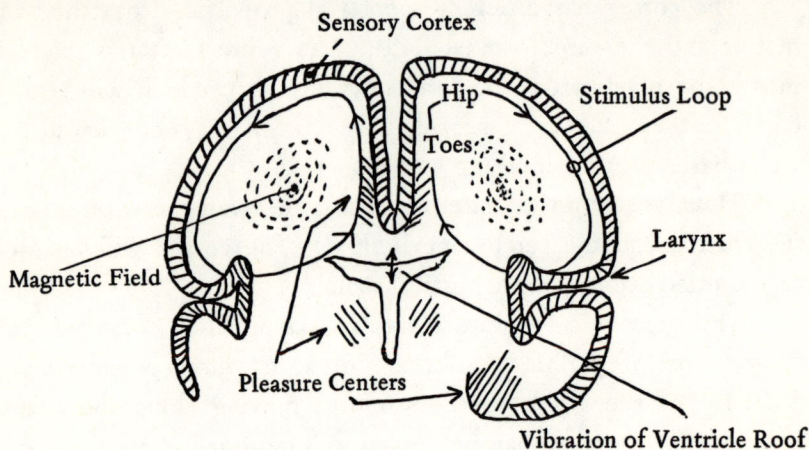

Figure 12. Frontal cross section of brain.

This is shown by EEG measurements, indicating that during meditation there are currents of opposing polarity, relative to the midline, flowing along the sensory cortex of both hemispheres. These occur in both the alpha and theta range of brain wave frequencies.

As the stimulus travels through, it crosses an area which contains a pleasure center. When the pleasure center is thus stimulated, the meditator experiences a state of ecstasy. To reach that state it may take years of systematic meditation, or again, in certain people it may happen spontaneously.

As long as the four oscillators (1) the aorta, (2) the heart sounds, (3) the standing waves in the ventricles, (4) the circulating sensory stimulus or kundalini current are in phase and resonating, all parts of the body move in harmony. The fifth oscillating circuit is activated when the sensory cortex tissue has been finally polarized to the point where there is a circulation of electrical current in the hemispheres and a magnetic field develops inside the core of each current ring, as shown in Figures 13 and 14 (2).

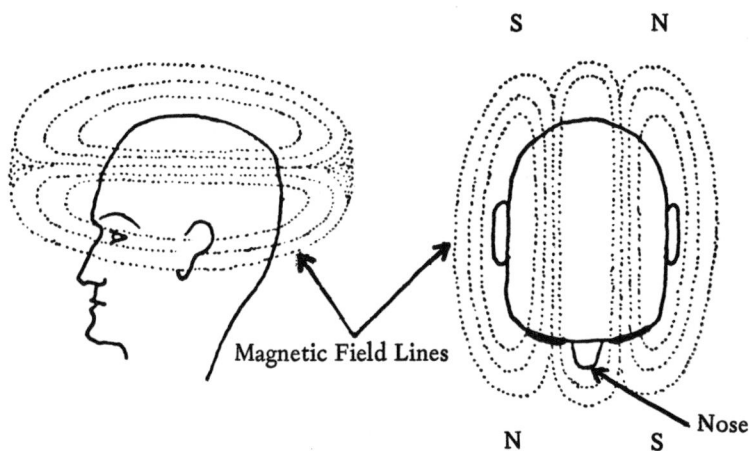

Figure 13.   Figure 14.
Lateral and top views of head, showing magnetic field lines.

This magnetic field pulsates in harmony with the other oscillators. The observed "normal" rate of the circulation of the sensory current is about 7 cycles/sec.

Pulsating magnetic fields of the order of 10^{-9} gauss are produced by the currents circulating in the brain. These currents may be detected by an electroencephalograph electrode on the skin surface of the head. However, they are quite variable (2). The sensory cortex currents will produce fields of symmetrical shape but with polarities associated with the two brain hemispheres opposing each other, as shown in Figures 13 and 14.

85

Thus by meditating in a quiet sitting position, we slowly activate 5 tuned oscillators. One by one these oscillators are locked into rhythm. This results eventually in the development of a pulsating magnetic field around the head. When this occurs, one may simultaneously observe other characteristic and automatic changes in the functioning of the nervous and circulatory systems. It is the purpose of meditation to bring about these changes in order to increase the ability of the nervous system to handle stress and overcome it more easily. The noise level in the nervous system is thus reduced, and the system becomes more efficient and permits a fuller development of the person's latent physical and mental capacities.

Any of the 5 tuned oscillators can be triggered individually after a short period of stimulation. Any one of them will get the sensory cortex current circulating and will soon lock the heart and the body's motion into an artificial state of meditation. This is a dangerous practice, which may be traumatic to an inexperienced meditator.

Subject	Pushed & pulled by field	pain & press. in head	press-ure in eyes	Stimulation in back of head	Pulse felt in neck	High-pitched sound in head	Press-ure in ears	Meditates
1	+				+			−
2		+				+		+
3		+	+		+			+
4			+		+			−
5	+							−
6	+							+
7	+	+	+					−
8		+	+	+				+
9						+	+	−
10	+							+
11		+						+
12	+	+		+	+			+
13		+		+	+	+		−
14	+							+
15	+	+						+
	8	8	4	3	5	3	1	

Table 1. Summary of responses of 15 subjects to unipolar 3.75-Hz, 0.5-gauss maximum intensity, 2-minute duration magnetic field stimulation applied to one hemisphere of the brain.

Magnetic Feedback

15 subjects sitting upright were subjected to hemispheric stimulation by an externally applied varying unipolar magnetic field of 0.5 gauss maximum intensity measured at the skin surface. The field was produced by a C-shaped electromagnet, with 30-cm pole gap spacing, activated by a voltage-offset sine wave power source, with frequency 3.75 Hz, and stimulus duration 2 minutes for each subject. The apparatus formed a closed magnetic circuit with lines of force going through the brain. The polarity of the applied field could be reversed. The responses of the subjects in a blind experiment were collected in tabular form. See Table 1.

More than 50 per cent of the subjects tested described sensations of pain or pressure in the head, also a sensation of being pushed and pulled by the applied magnetic field. These results suggest an interaction of the field around the head with the externally applied field.

Discussion

The symptom-sign of this "sensory-motor cortex syndrome", or what has been characterized as the kundalini process in ancient literature can be quite variable and sporadic. Its complete presentation usually begins as a transient paresthesia of the toes or ankle with numbness and tingling. Occasionally, there is diminished sensitivity to touch or pain, or even partial paralysis of the foot or leg. The process most frequently begins on the left side and ascends in a sequential manner from foot, leg, hip, to involve completely the left side of the body, including the face. Once the hip is involved, it is not uncommon to experience an intermittent throbbing or rhythmic rumbling-like sensation in the lower lumbar and sacral spine. This is followed by an ascending sensation which rises along the spine to the cervical and occipital regions of the head.

At these latter areas, severe pressure-caused occipital headaches and cervical neck aches may be experienced at times. These pressures, usually transient but occasionally persistent, may also be felt anywhere along the spine, right or left side of chest, different parts of the head and the eyes. Some individuals will notice tingling sensations descending along the face to the laryngeal areas. The tracheolaryngeal region may also be felt as a sudden rushing of air to and fro. Respiration may become spasmodic with involuntarily occurring maximum expirations. Various auditory tones have been noted, from constant low pitched hums to high pitched ringing. Visual aberrations and temporary decrease or loss of vision has been observed. The sequence of symptoms continues later down into the lower abdominal region.

Because a particular symptom or sign of the altered sensory and motor systems may occur or persist for months or years, the sequence of symptoms may not be obvious, nor appear causally connected. Also, only in a few of the known cases will all of the symptoms in this sequence become vividly apparent to each person. Normally, physical and laboratory examination reveals either little or no pathology and therefore, except in rare cases, many of the complaints are probably dismissed as psychosomatic or neurotic symptoms.

Meditation has been considered, here and elsewhere, as a stress removal process (14, 16). The symptoms noted above are indications that release of stress is taking place. Stress, as defined by H. Selye, is "a state manifested by a specific syndrome which consists of all the nonspecifically induced changes within a biological system" (16). The intensity of the symptoms is an index of the severity of the stress being released. On the whole, these symptoms should be looked upon as a positive sign of normalization of the body. The unusual aspect of this mechanism is that the release of stress is experienced as a localized stimulation of a particular part of the body, as opposed to the accepted notion that stress is a diffuse general state.

A large percentage of individuals who meditate and who have previously used psychedelic drugs for extended periods of time, or are experiencing unusual stress, are more likely to show these symptoms. These will eventually subside by themselves, without the need for any medical intervention.

It is the spontaneously triggered cases that present a problem, since the individual does not know the cause of these symptoms, and tends to panic. The psychological problems may mimic schizophrenia, and be diagnosed as such by the physician. As a consequence, drastic procedures may be used to alleviate the problem.

An awareness of the existence of the above-noted symptoms and the mechanism which triggers them is important, in view of the constantly increasing number of persons practicing meditation, and therefore likely to experience these effects of stress release.

Possible Rhythm Entrainment Effects

Our experiments show that when a person in deep meditation is suddenly called to come out and stop meditating, the normal response is reluctance to abandon that state and a lapsing back into deep meditation repeatedly. This seems to suggest that a "locking in" situation is present. It is well-known that the larger the number of frequency-locked oscillators in a system, the more stable the system and the more difficult it is to disturb.

When a situation exists, where there are two oscillators vibrating at frequencies close to each other, the oscillator which is operating at a higher frequency will usually lock into step the slower oscillator. This is rhythm entrainment. When in the state of deep meditation, a person goes into sine wave oscillation at approximately 7 cycles/sec, there is a tendency for him or her to be locked into the frequency of the planet (Figure 15).

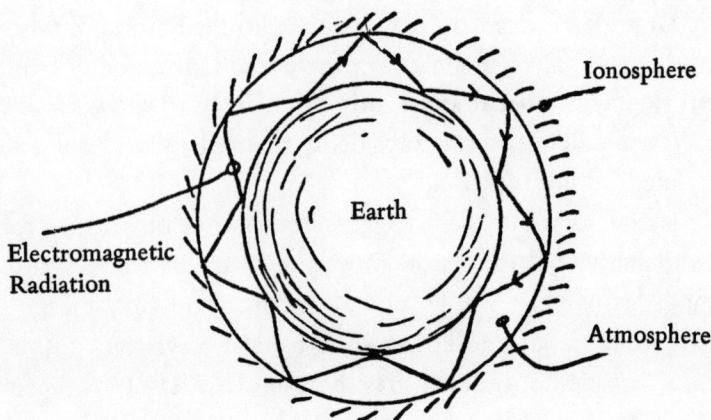

Figure 15. The Earth's atmosphere is shown as a resonant cavity.

We have talked about resonant cavities and how a stimulus can set such a cavity vibrating at its own resonant frequency. Our planet has a conductive layer around it called ionosphere, which starts about 80 km from the earth's surface. The cavity between the earth and the ionosphere (the atmosphere) is also a resonant cavity. Certain types of electromagnetic radiation travel through this cavity, being reflected alternately between the Earth's surface and the ionosphere, and vibrate at characteristic resonant frequencies.

In 1957, W. O. Schumann (19, 22) calculated the earth-ionosphere cavity resonance frequencies at 10.6, 18.3, and 25.9 Hz. More recent work by J. Toomey and C. Polk (1970) (22) gave the values 7.8, 14.1, 20.3 26.4 and 32.5 Hz. The lowest frequency, 7.8 Hz, is approximately equal to the velocity of electromagnetic radiation divided by the earth's circumference:

$$\frac{2.998 \times 10^8 \text{ m/sec}}{4.003 \times 10^7 \text{ m}} = 7.489 \text{ or } 7.5 \text{ Hz}$$

This is the reciprocal of the time required for a beam of electromagnetic radiation to go around the earth.

The planet is very much affected and quite closely coupled by its plasma fields with the sun. These two bodies and their interacting fields form our immediate environment. The sun produces energy in a wide spectrum, from powerful X-rays to acoustical signals (8, 9). The solar wind shapes the magnetosphere and the plasma-spheres of our planet. All these layers contain charged particles produced by the sun. In the Van Allen belts, these particles oscillate back and forth along the magnetic lines of the earth between the north and the south poles. Much of this vibration occurs in the frequency range 1 to 40 Hz, well within physiological frequencies (18).

There is a strong coupling between these oscillations and the changes in the magnetic field of the earth. These microfluctuations of the magnetic field are on the order of 10^{-5} gauss, about 10,000 times stronger than the fields around our heads. We live within this constantly active natural electro-magnetic environment, with the added perturbations of broadcasting TV and radio stations (15).

Given these conditions, it would be reasonable to assume that the fluctuations in these planetary environmental fields have affected human evolution in subtle ways over the ages—in ways which are not quite clear to us yet (15).

Our knowledge of physiology considers the present state of the human nervous system as being at the peak of its development. However, this article suggests a mechanism which may cause changes in the cerebrospinal system. When a fetus develops in the womb, it undergoes changes, which mirror human evolution from a fish through the amphibian to the mammal. But our findings suggest that this evolution very probably has not come to a halt with the way our present nervous system is presently functioning. The hidden potential of our nervous system may be vast.

The mechanism outlined above describes a possible next step in the evolution of the nervous system, which can be accelerated by the use of certain techniques. We can speculate that this development will have the effect of an increased awareness of the self as a part of a much larger system. We can postulate that our magnetic "antennae" will bring in information about our extended system—the planet and the sun—and will allow us to interpret geophysical phenomena and signals to better advantage (1).*

---

* Reference 1 shows that one of the orientation mechanisms of the homing pigeon depends on the magnetic fields of the earth. Indications are that the pigeon's built-in magnetic field is interacting with the earth's magnetic field. The pigeon's field would be analogous to the magnetic field around our head, when intensified by the sensory cortex "current".

ACKNOWLEDGEMENTS

The author thanks Earl Ettienne, Ph.D., of Harvard Medical School, Richard P. Ingrasci, M. D., of Boston State Hospital, and William A. Tiller, Ph.D., of Stanford University, for their help in reviewing the article and for many valuable suggestions.

Special thanks are due to Paul Nardella of Easton, Massachusetts for his design and construction of the electronic equipment used in making the measurements described in this report.

REFERENCES

1. C. Walcott, R. Green, "Orientation of Homing Pigeons Altered by a Change in the Direction of an Applied Magnetic Field", *Science,* vol. 184, no. 4133, 12 April 1974.

2. D. Cohen, "Magnetoencephalograph: Detection of the Brain's Electrical Activity with a Superconducting Magnetometer", *Science*, vol. 175, no. 4022, 11 February 1972.

3. A. Weissler, *Non-Invasive Cardiology,* chapter on ballistocardiography, Grune & Stratton, New York, 1974.

4. K. Wallace, H. Benson, "The Physiology of Meditation", *Scientific American,* February 1972.

5. D. Bergel, *Cardio-Vascular Fluid Dynamics,* chapter 10, Academic Press, New York, 1972.

6. P. New, "Arterial Stationary Waves", *American Journal of Roentgenology,* vol. 97, no. 2, p. 488-499.

7. T. Ruch, H. Patton, J. Woodbury, A. Towe, *Neurophysiology,* 1st edition, p. 262, Saunders Publishing Co., Philadelphia, 1962.

8. D. Thomsen, "On the Edge of Space", *Science News,* vol. 94, no. 9, p. 216, 31 August 1968.

9. A. Ewing, "The Noisy Sun", "Ion Signals Across Space", *Science News,* vol. 92, no. 11, p. 250, 9 September 1967.

10. M. Gauquelin, *The Cosmic Clocks,* Avon Books, New York 1974.

11. R. Bucke, *Cosmic Consciousness,* E. P. Dutton & Co., New York, 1970.

12. G. Krishna, *Higher Consciousness,* Julian Press Inc., New York, 1974.

13. J. Banquet, "Electroencephalography and Clinical Neurophysiology", *EEG and Meditation,* vol. 33, p. 454, 1972.

14. H. Benson, *The Relaxation Response,* Wm. Morrow & Co., New York, 1975.

15. R. Becker, "Electromagnetic Forces and Life Processes", *M. I. T. Technology Review,* vol. 75, no. 2, p. 32, December 1972.

16. H. Selye, *The Stress of Life,* McGraw-Hill, New York, 1956.

17. C. Tart, *Altered States of Consciousness,* John Wiley & Sons, New York, 1969.

18. H. Konig, "Biological Effects of Low Frequency Electrical Phenomena", *Interdisciplinary Cycle Research,* vol. 2, no. 3, 1971.

19. W. Schumann, "Electrische Eigenshwingungen des Hohlraumes Erde-Luft-Ionosphere", *Zeitschrift fur Angewandte Physik,* vol. 9, pp. 373-378 1957.

20. A. Luisada, *The Sounds of the Normal Heart,* Warren H. Green Publishing Co., St. Louis, 1972.

21. Col. J. P. Stapp, "The "G" Spectrum in Space Flight Dynamics", *Lectures in Aerospace Medicine,* 16-20 January 1961.

22. M. Persinger, ed., *ELF and VLF Electromagnetic Field Effects,* Plenum Press, New York, 1974.

APPENDIX B

MASTS: THE GOD-INTOXICATED ONES

Masts is the name used by Meher Baba to refer to "God-intoxicated" people, "mutants" towards a primal link with the Divine. They seem to arise in times of stress to fulfill certain vital functions for the benefit of humankind.

Because of the strangeness of their behavior they may easily be mistaken for psychotics. However, their condition may be distinguished from schizophrenia, by their compelling attractiveness to the ordinary folk who gather around to serve and be near them, and a recognition of them as saints by their followers. They have an obvious lack of interest in dealing with ordinary life situations, their own physical needs, emotional relationships, or even intellectual functioning in the ordinary sense. Meher Baba worked with both Masts and psychotics, and distinguished between the two. He made no effort to cure them. His labors with them were never defined by him and must remain obscure.

The Masts seem to appear only within a solid religious tradition. It was believed by Donkin, the physician who studied and accompanied Meher Baba for years, that they served as pivotal points for intervention, forces in themselves, around which, and through whom, other spiritual influences could work to serve humanity. Their power seemed to him more autonomous and primal than that of the mind, heart, or spirit of other Holy persons.

Such saintly ones have not, to our knowledge, appeared yet in the West. However, with the strengthening of all sorts of religious tendencies here now, and the worsening world crisis, they could begin to appear here.

The rebirth process of kundalini awakening at times evokes similar feelings and behavior to those of the Masts. In fact, it is just in this way that Masts may be born. If that does happen in this country, someone will surely have these gentle saints referred to our clinics, then what will we do?

96

APPENDIX C

SENSITIVITY IN THE HUMAN ORGANISM

The basis for all creativity is sensitivity of the physical organism. This is developed on a regular schedule of unfolding, from infancy to adulthood, if nothing negative intervenes to stop it. In due time, as we leave the sheltering environment of our early home-life, this growing sensitivity brings us in tune with the great world outside. Ideally we also contact our own inner reality and processes so our responsiveness becomes self-aware, not only intuitively tuned in, but also solidly rooted in mature understanding.

The conceptual orientation should properly be a later addition, but never a substitute, for instinctive ways of being in touch with the world around us. The intuitive harmony is our natural animal heritage. It can be seen in the remarkable ability of dogs and horses to sense the needs or whereabouts of their trainers when the latter are far distant. Many animals are now known to prepare in advance for floods, earthquakes, and other natural disasters, which commonly catch people today by surprise. In Appendix A, Bentov has suggested that magnetic fields around the head, generated by the effects of kundalini, could enable a human being to orient himself or herself to planetary and solar electromagnetic fluctuations in a way similar to that achieved now by pigeons and other migratory birds.

In our studies we have observed the development of these intuitive powers as a difficult and painful rebirth occurring later in life, and even then only in rare individuals. But in certain primitive tribes such as the bushmen and aborigines these abilities develop easily and naturally from childhood onwards. Why should people in the West need two births to claim this natural birthright? This suggests that the intuitive mechanism must be reborn because it has in the meantime "died"—or, to put it bluntly, it has been killed.

Rather than genetic inheritance alone being necessary for the development of this sensitivity, negative environmental factors must also be avoided or dealt with to preserve and enhance this process. In the West, factors encountered before birth and continuously thereafter, act to curtail the growth of human feelings (Pearce, 1976). In the sensitive human organism, with proper protection of the psyche in its early development, the kundalini cycle begins easily and normally. But with inherent weaknesses present, and negative factors in the ascendency, the organism becomes overwhelmed. Each system and function probably has its own natural time to become activated and grow at a pace determined from within in order to ensure the harmonious development of the whole child. But our culture cuts off the tender shoots of the delicate plant of feeling with the cold hard sharpness of mechanical insensitivity, while on the other hand forcefeeding fertilizer and vitamins to the barely sprouted seedling of conceptual thought. The entire system is thrown out of balance, and harmonious development stops. (Pearce, 1976, has suggested that children should not be taught to read until the age of ten).

In some, the result is the breakdown in the thought and feeling processes known as schizophrenia. In others, physical symptoms and disease results. In the more resistant, a hardening occurs and they may become depressed. They lose touch with their inner emotional world, and show hardening of the heart, becoming tough and unresponsive to both outer and inner worlds, then emotionally petrified and senile.

However, vestiges of the feeling process are detectable in the theta-delta activity of the brainwaves which, though normally subdued in the waking state, are seen in certain sleep stages. Thus this one manifestation of feeling or intuitive activity can be curtailed in our conscious self, but never extinguished in the subconscious.

If death of the feeling mechanism is brought about in part by the stress of emotional insensitivity and too early conceptualization on the young child by a mechanized environment, what then brings about its rebirth in later life?

One way to increase the responsiveness of the five senses is by fasting. This causes a predictable increase in the senses of touch, smell, taste, hearing, and vision, which occurs as an automatic response of the biological mechanism. There is an increased sensitivity to internal stimuli, as well as to the world outside. This is shown by the greater incidence of seeing visions and or hearing internal voices that often becomes possible.

Fasting in the normal or schizophrenic state adds stress to the organism. This inner crisis acts similarly to external crisis states to bring the organism back to its senses. The impact of reality becomes more tangible and immediate, hence more successful in moving the organism towards behavior consonant with this new view of reality.

Stress, in general, prepares the person to see the real for what it is, and sets the biological organism into an increased readiness, physically and mentally, to meet the emergency situation and survive. In other words, it is stress later in life that is necessary to shock the organism into a return to the feeling self, which was overwhelmed by too great a stress early in life. The conceptual mechanism was better able than the still undeveloped feeling mechanism to deal with the social crisis imposed in infancy, but in the end the organism has to return to the feeling system to cope with the more basic needs of a biological crisis of fasting, war, or other life-and-death situations.

To cope with all types of stress and its results, a coming to know oneself, is one of the more efficient ways. So one turns to a discipline, or teacher, or Guru, focusing on spiritual development, hopefully from a strong position of stability and understanding. Most of us do not turn within to ask for answers, unless forced to do so by a failure of the outer world to satisfy and protect. To become consonant, resonant with nature within and without, is the goal; that to which we must return in order to "become as little children". The kundalini force tunes us to our cosmos within and to the cosmos without as well.

APPENDIX D

FOR PHYSICIANS AND NEUROLOGISTS

There are a number of medical disorders that may develop some of the symptoms of the complex we have been discussing. These generally are no problem for a well-trained diagnostician. However, the two young women who saw neurologists had symptoms that were converted to more serious manifestations because of their ignorance and fear, augmented by some perplexity on the part of their physicians. It is not feasible in this book to discuss the many neurological disorders which could be considered. Instead, we will use one rather obscure disorder as a model for the whole class that displays motor, sensory, and febrile changes which may appear in the kundalini complex as well.

Icelandic Disease

Icelandic disease (Roueche, 1965) is probably of virus nature, has an acute onset characterized by pains in the neck and back, paresthesias and hyperesthesias (extremes of skin sensitivity), muscle weakness (as in polio), paresis, nervousness, insomnia, loss of memory, and terrifying dreams. Those struck are usually persons in their twenties and thirties. It is never fatal. Some of the cases show pain in the arms and back and legs, as well as headaches. There may also be delirium during the day, sensations of imbalance, and strange feelings in the legs. Other reported tingling and sweating in the hands and feet, ringing in the ears, and confusion. All these symptoms may be noted in our physio-kundalini complex cases.

The victims are more often women than men, and the epidemics tend to strike members of isolated or closed communities. Occasionally the emotional overlay of tension, anxiety, and depression are quite marked. The disorder has a prolonged and relapsing course which may last for a year or more. It is notable that none of the areas of paresthesias corresponded to any recognized area innervated by nerves.

The specialists in these cases were so confused by this array of signs and symptoms that the "bughouse possibility actually occurred to us . . . the more of their complaints we heard the more we began to wonder about a functional (neurotic) explanation." (Roueche, 1965, p. 216).

One of the patients even experienced internal vibrations as if she was shaking all over inside. This '. a common symptom in our cases.

This disorder has received several names. Among the most familiar are Icelandic disease, acute infective encephalomyelitis, atypical poliomyelitis and epidemic̆ neuromyasthenia. I have seen one case of this disorder in a meditator and thought seriously, for a time, that this young woman might be in the throes of the physio-kundalini complex.

The only symptom these cases do not report that ours do is seeing light internally. However, these patients would have to be re-questioned to be sure that this symptom is actually missing. A physician would no more think of asking about such a possibility than a teacher of yoga would consider measuring the temperature of the reported hot areas of his students' bodies.

APPENDIX E

QUESTIONS FOR RESEARCH PARTICIPANTS

The following questions have been formulated as a guide to physicians and researchers exploring the psychotic-like states that may accompany physio-kundalini processes. We are particularly interested in detailed descriptions of your pure sensory experience rather than interpretations of these unusual events. Those who wish to do so are encouraged to send case history information, including birth date, time, and place to Lee Sannella, M.D., 3101 Washington Street, San Francisco, CA 94115. Include descriptions of other psychic experiences such as psychokinetic effects, clairvoyance, ESP, etc. Please send a stamped self-addressed envelope and your telephone number if you would like a reply.

1. Do you hear sounds such as tones, music, hissing, roaring, thunder, drumming, or the sound of cymbals when no such sounds are produced outside your head? Do the sounds *seem* to come from inside or outside your head?

2. Do you have visualizations or visual hallucinations? Do you experience light inside your head or body, or see the environment as illuminated by other than normal means? What color are the lights, how bright are they, and of how long duration? Do they have a particular form?

3. Do you sense unusual heat or cold in your body or on your skin? Does it move from place to place or stay in one area? Is there any objective evidence of temperature change (can it be measured by a thermometer)? If so, for how long at a time, how often, and how large are these temperature changes?

4. Do you have sensations of tickling, tingling, vibrating, itching, crawling, pleasant or unpleasant, within the body or on the skin? Do these move around in a patterned manner? Are the movements bilaterally symmetrical? Where do they start and to where do they move? Please note especially if they start in the legs and move toward the back, neck, head, and face, in that order.

5. Are there spontaneous involuntary positioning of the limbs, fingers, or body? Are there jerky, smooth, sinuous, rhythmic, spasmodic, or violent, involuntary body movements? Do you ever inadvertently cry out, grunt, yell, or scream? Do you ever stare into space for long periods of time or appear wild-eyed? Are there odd breathing patterns at times? If so, do these last experiences occur most often when you are alone, sitting quietly, or in bed?

REFERENCES

T. Agpaoa, Personal Communication, 1974.

H. Andrade, S. Hashizume, G. Playfair, "Recurrent Patterns in RSPK Cases", *Second International Congress on Psychotronic Research,* Monte Carlo, 1975. Proceedings of IAPR available from Secretariat of IAPR, 43 Eglinton Ave., East, Suite 803, Toronto, Canada M4P1A2.

B. Bhavan, *Sufis, Mystics and Yogis of India,* Bankey Behari, Bombay, 1971.

Holy Bible, King James Version, Luke 11:34.

D. Brenner, S. Williamson, L. Kaufman, "Visually Evoked Magnetic Fields of the Human Brain", *Science,* October 31, 1975.

R. Bucke, *Cosmic Consciousness*, E. P. Dutton & Co., Inc., New York, 1970.

J. Campbell, *The Mythic Image,* Princeton University Press, Princeton, 1974.

C. Castaneda, *The Teachings of Don Juan,* Ballantine Books, New York, 1968.

F. Courtois, *An Experience of Enlightenment,* Shunju-Sha, Tokyo, 1970.

W. Donkin, *The Wayfarers,* A. Irani, Maharashtra, India, 1948.

A. Greeley, W. McCready, "Are We a Nation of Mystics?" *New York Times Magazine Section,* January 26, 1975.

A. Green, paper presented at the *Transpersonal Psychology Conference,* Stanford University, July, 1975.

W. James, *The Varieties of Religious Experience,* New American Library, New York, 1958.

G. Jonas, "Manfred Clynes and the Science of Sentics", *Saturday Review,* May 13, 1972.

C. Jung, J. Hauer, *Kundalini Yoga,* unpublished manuscript, 1932.

C. Jung, *Civilization in Transition*, Bollingen Series X, New York, 1964.

C. Jung, *Psychological Commentary on Kundalini Yoga*, Spring, 1975.

R. Katz, "Education for Transcendence: Lessons from the !Kung Zhu Twasi", *Journal of Transpersonal Psychology*, November 2, 1973.

G. Krishna, *Kundalini: The Evolutionary Energy in Man*, Shambhala, Berkeley, 1971.

G. Krishna, "The True Aim of Yoga", *Psychic*, January/February, 1973.

G. Krishna, "Science and Kundalini", paper presented at the *Seminar on Yoga, Science and Man*, New Delhi, 1975.

C. Luk, *The Secrets of Chinese Meditation*, Samuel Weiser, Inc., New York, 1972.

C. Luk, *Taoist Yoga*, Samuel Weiser, New York, 1973.

M. Manning, *The Link*, Holt, Rinehart, and Winston, New York, 1975.

J. Millay, personal communication, 1976.

R. Monroe, *Journeys Out of the Body*, Doubleday, Garden City, 1971.

F. Morris, "Exorcising the Devil in California", *Fate*, July and August, 1974.

F. Morris, *Self-Hypnosis in Two Days*, E. P. Dutton and Co., Inc., New York, 1975.

S. Muktananda, *The Play of Consciousness*, Shree Gurudev Ashram, Campbell, CA, 1974.

S. Muktananda, personal communication, 1975.

S. Narayanananda, *The Primal Power in Man*, Prasad and Company, Rishkesh, India, 1960.

W. Penfield, *The Excitable Cortex in Conscious Man*, Charles C. Tomas, Springfield, Ill, 1958.

J. Pearce, *The Magical Child*, to be published by E. P. Dutton and Co., Inc., 1976.

P. Rohrbach, *The Search for St. Therese*, Dell, New York, 1963.

B. Roueche, "Annals of Medicine in the Bughouse", *The New Yorker*, November 27, 1965.

D. Roy, I. Devi, *Pilgrims of the Stars*, Dell Publishing Company, New York, 1974.

K. Seo, personal communication, 1974.

J. Skutch, personal communication, 1974.

V. Tirtha, *Devatma Shakti*, Delhi, 1962.

C. Walcott, R. Green, "Orientation of Homing Pigeons Altered by a Change in the Direction of Applied Magnetic Fields", *Science*, April 12, 1974.

R. Dobrin, C. Kirsch, S. Kirsch, J. Pierrakos, E. Schwartz, T. Wolff, Y. Zeira, "Experimental Measurements of the Human Energy Field", in S. Krippner and D. Rubin (editors), *The Energies of Consciousness*, Gordon and Breach, New York, 1975.

INDEX

INDEX

genetic or natural, 43, 51, 59, 65, 98
genius, 6, 31
Gospels, 49
15, 31
Great Body, 19, 22, 50, 53
Greeley, A., 2
Greene, A., 50
headaches (also head pressures), 16-58, 87-88
healing, 14, 17, 25, 35-38
heat or burning, 1, 14-25, 28-36, 40-46, 52-57, 66, 67
and vibrations, 19
Hillman, J., 24
hysteria, 16, 46, 48, 64, 88, 101
Icelandic disease, 100
impurities, see blocks
insane feelings, 21, 28, 32, 48, 60, 63, 65
James, W., 9, 24, 64
Jesus, 30, 50
Jonas, G., 67
Jung, C. G., 6, 7, 9, 33, 35, 40, 49-50
Kalahari, 14, 60
Katz, R., 14-15
Korean, 19
Krishna, G., 2, 4, 6-7, 20, 21
kundalini
    arising or awakening of, 4, 6, 9-12, 51-64, 71, 83
    arrest, 33, 40
    as an impersonal force, 6, 7
    classical, 4-9, 11-20, 55-56, 71
    complications of, 22
    dangers of, 14-64, 86
    definition, 4, 6, 7, 11, 71, 87
    lower and higher bodies, 30
    medical intervention, 23, 38, 89
    modification of, 28, 30, 34, 58-59, 63, 66, 89

physical maturity and, 30-31
    resistance to, see blocks
    signs and symptoms, 4, 10, 14-22, 44-54, 102-103
    sudden or spontaneous, 14-42, 62, 64, 75, 89
    (as) therapy, 33, 41-42, 56, 58-59, 61-64
    triggering of, 22, 51, 56, 71-72, 89
Kundalini Research Foundation, 7
!Kung, 14-15
light, 18-67, 101-102
Luk, C., 18
magnetic stimulation, 37, 41, 54, 86-87
    in a psychic, 41
Maharshi, R., 30
Manning, M., 29
Masts, 5, 60, 65, 96
Meher Baba, 5, 60, 96
meditation, 7-66, 71-88
    artificial, 81
    locked in, 39, 89
    spontaneous, 39, 84
Millay, J., 67
Morris, F., 17
Motoyama, H., 66, 68
Muktananda, Swami, 13, 20-21, 41, 48, 55, 61, 62, 63
myelogram, 38-39
Narayanananda, 20
neurological evolution or development, 4, 6, 73, 86, 91-92, 96
Nikkhilananda, 20
n'um, 14-15
orgasm, see sex
Osiris, 25, 37, 49
out-of-body, 50, 51, 54, 68
pain, 18-66, 87, 100
paralysis, 39-40, 46, 51, 87
paresthesias, 83, 87, 100, 101

NOTES